Thoughts on Unity
wholeness and the end of suffering

by

Todd Lorentz

Vedanta Publishing
Edmonton, Canada

Thoughts On Unity:
wholeness and the end of suffering
Copyright © 2018

by Todd Lorentz

All rights reserved.
Printed in the United States of America.

ISBN: 978-0-9877782-3-9

First Edition, February 2018

Published by Vedanta Publishing
Edmonton, Canada
www.VedantaPublishing.com

This book is dedicated to
Benjamin Creme.
I am deeply grateful to have
had the opportunity to receive
so much from his humour, his
wisdom and his encouragement.

The creation of this book on unity began as a project in autumn of 2016 and for more than a year I worked on bringing many of the ideas that I had accumulated over the years together with a wide range of thoughts that I had developed for myself. The incredible importance of unity only revealed itself to me more fully once I had the opportunity to gather all of these thoughts into one coherent format. It has been an engaging and provocative book to write and I hope that it will help to generate a new appreciation for the significance and consequence of unity.

There were many along the way who gave of their time, labour and support to make this work come together. Thanks should go to the staff and owners of our community gathering place, the Juniper Bistro, for their support and encouragement. I would also like to thank Olga for her help in designing the cover. More than anyone, though, I would like to thank Heather for her eternal willingness to help with transcription and proofreading, her assistance through the endless editing process and for being a sounding board for my many thoughts and ideas. Her selflessness and dedication are evidence of the divinity in us all.

Todd Lorentz
Edmonton, February 2018

Table of Contents

Introduction...1

Wholeness and the Nature of Reality..............7

The Origins of Separation............................24

The Illusion of Separation............................47

The Illusion of Identity................................64

Dis-unity and Suffering................................92

Unity and Language...................................101

Unity and Individuality..............................114

The Economics of Unity: Sharing...............133

Unity: The Way Forward for Humanity.......166

Unity and the End of Suffering...................174

A human being is a part of the whole called by us universe, a part limited in time and space. He experiences himself, his thoughts and feeling as something separated from the rest, a kind of optical delusion of his consciousness. This delusion is a kind of prison for us, restricting us to our personal desires and to affection for a few persons nearest to us. Our task must be to free ourselves from this prison by widening our circle of compassion to embrace all living creatures and the whole of nature in its beauty.

– Albert Einstein

Introduction

All things are one.

– *Chuang Tzu*

Humanity is divine, and every human being in that family is One through the medium of that divinity. It is a bold claim when viewed through the lens of everyday material living. Yet countless teachers throughout the ages have made this very same pronouncement. Even more tenuous seems the claim when one measures the ocean of suffering within which humanity swims, looking for even the slightest glimmer of relief from its endless struggle. Poverty and scarcity consume the hope of many while famine, war, hunger, disease, displacement and fear destroy the very fabric of trust and goodwill. Greed, corruption, injustice and competition stand out as common practice within the political, economic and religious institutions of the world. How is one to reconcile this dichotomy?

Mystics and sages have repeatedly stepped forward from within the ranks of humankind to proclaim the high stature and divine gifts which are the privilege of every woman and man to express. Throughout the ages, and against our apparent determin-

Introduction

ation to the contrary, we have managed to achieve ever higher expressions of divinity in the form of creativity, civility and invention. Each divine attribute, achieved and then added to the complex of human expression, has come at enormous cost to those courageous enough to meet the challenge and has sometimes even led to the destruction of entire civilisations. From the ashes of each society rises the phoenix of ever greater liberation; out of ignorance we discover higher measures of justice, broader understandings of human capacity and more profound capacities for self-awareness. The evolution of consciousness through the human form is beset with challenges – fraught with pain and suffering. Yet, that burgeoning consciousness inspires and informs each new civilisation toward an ever greater reformation and salvation of mankind.

There is no return for humanity to the origins of evolution. Nor is there any clear understanding of our ultimate goal or destination. Humanity has stumbled forward relentlessly in the dark, gathering whatever small bits of advice it can along the road from those few Great Souls who have penetrated the darkness and shed light upon the Way for others to follow. Those Illumined Minds have paved smoother the rocky path which is our collective journey and have bestowed a route promising the end of suffering for those who would study those signs and apply themselves toward quickening their own pace.

A number of teachings from antiquity have shown a multitude of ways to bring the man or woman to evolution's bright conclusion. If one can catch a glimpse of the larger story, vast differences of approach can be seen to fuse and merge into a divine symphony of common purpose and goal.

I have always been provoked by the faint, yet palpable, sense of unity in the world. I have come to learn that this fascination is not uncommon and I've had the good fortune to meet many people who share in this familiar intuition. Despite this, my daily experience has been saturated by the perceptions of an objectively material world existence and that we function as separate and distinct individuals in the material world. Every one of my senses, which largely govern the *way* I experience the world, works to undermine my subjective sense of unity and inclusiveness at every breath. I have wanted to dive more deeply into that vast space of 'belongingness', yet I am often prohibited from entering fully into that reality by the monotonous distractions which infiltrate the mind at every turn – conditioned as it is by its reflexive identification with the outer objective world. This challenging circumstance has led me on a prolonged journey of investigation to understand the relationship between the objective and subjective world, and to study the advice and teachings from

Introduction

various mystical, philosophical and religious traditions. I have hoped to better understand why these two worlds, the subjective and the objective, can often yield such diverse and sometimes incompatible presentations of reality. Moreover, I have sought to understand how this relates to the experience we call suffering and how the great sages of the past have managed to penetrate and overcome that deep mystery.

The many views that I have had the opportunity to examine have exemplified the idea of nonduality as a fundamental condition of the universe. Nonduality is the view that there is "not two". That is, while we appear to live in a world that is full of various independent objects and beings, nonduality is the view that there is no true separation between subjects and objects. There is no independently existing entity called "you" and "me", although "you" and "me" certainly *appear* to exist as two distinct beings. We are really better described as two distinct expressions of one underlying consciousness of Being. The common analogy of this is the image of the ocean with many white caps or waves on the surface. You can see each individual wave in each its own unique form and expression but underneath the surface they are all part of the same one ocean. There is no way to separate the 'waves' from the 'ocean'. In short, the world (or ocean) is One. We each make a separate and distinct appearance in

Introduction

the world but underneath, in the field of consciousness, we are all part of the same waters of divine life.

This led me to think for many years on the relationship between this underlying unity of Being and how we manifest our lives singularly and separately in the material world. While our activities appear so individual, and individually motivated, we can't really separate that from the ocean of life any more than the wave can separate itself from the body of water from which it arises. And yet, the mass of humanity functions in the world today 'as if' there was no real connection to one another, nature or to the divine life that lies behind all of existence. As I pondered upon the effect that this schism has in our lives I began to see how essential the need was to not only recover that sense of unity but how critical it was to establish unity as a central demonstration in every aspect of living. It begs the question, if our fundamental nature is Oneness then how can we expect to flourish in any meaningful way without the basic expression of that unity in our daily lives? I look out at the world in its present state of endless wars, widespread hunger and poverty, mass refugee movements, collapse of entire ecosystems and the toxic economic gulf which exists between the 'haves' and the 'have-nots' – brought about by systems of competition, greed and selfishness – and it becomes clear to me how precarious life on

Introduction

our planet becomes when we abandon the principles of unity as a manifestation of what defines us.

These chapters comprise a few of my thoughts on unity and the fundamental role that it has in our lives. The challenges ahead of us seem great and, yet, we should know that building a world based on unity is one of the most natural things that we could do. It is in our nature to do this. It also requires that we begin to deconstruct the rationales and silly aphorisms that have been used to convince us that our best way forward is to continue through isolation, alienation, separation, competition and self-promotion. Instead, the route of unity leads us to sharing, cooperation, justice, synthesis, brotherhood and Love. I have hope that my thoughts here on the significance of unity can find a dominant place in your life as well.

Wholeness and the Nature of Reality

> All life is energy. If that energy is allowed to glow without any contradiction, without any friction, without any conflict, then that energy is boundless, endless.
>
> – *Krishnamurti*

The notion of an ultimate nondual reality has been around as long as we have recorded the thoughts and beliefs of civilised humanity. Stretching far back in history, and continuing forward into the various religious and spiritual perspectives today, we see beliefs grounded in the wholistic union between the spiritual and the material worlds. The primary expression of this perspective is called *pantheism*, where all existence is considered to be a literal manifestation of God. God does not exist outside of creation but, instead, is inherent in every atom of the cosmos. The world *is* God. Everything from nature to the forces that govern the cosmos – and including humans as well – is an expression of the manifested body of God. The adherents of this view are found throughout history from the early Hindu and Buddhist writers, through many of the Greek philosophers, across virtually all of the mystery traditions (Elusian, Hermetic, Gnostic, Sufi, Kabbalah and more) and even including more modern western thinkers as Spinoza and Einstein. The list is extensive.

In a turn of thinking, the pantheistic view evolved in a way that made God not only present in creation but also existent beyond the limitations of time and space. Described as *panentheism*, creation is imbued with God's life as the prime driver while, at the same time, God remains mysteriously outside of creation and unencumbered by the world's imperfections. On Its own plane God could be seen as remaining perfect and unencumbered. Creation became more of an "emanation" of the divine rather than the actual manifestation of God Itself. This view also played an important role in the development of many eastern and western religions, was adopted amongst various sects in some of the mystery traditions, and also provided an explanatory role for some western philosophers, such as Hegel and Whitehead, in bridging the gap between the empirical and religious worlds. However, this separation between God and its creation raises some problems in that it implies a relationship of necessity which works in both directions. That is, one can say that the world needs God in order for it to be created. However, it must also be reasoned that God needs the world in order to instantiate or authenticate Its existence. In simpler terms, the existence of God depends upon the existence of the world, and vise versa. Not only does this generate an internal contradiction (a tautology) but it contradicts mainstream Christian and Islamic theism and the doctrine of *creation ex nihilo* ("creation out of nothing"). In those modern theistic views, God is thoroughly independent of its creation and exists whether or not "the world" exists. Likewise, God is free to create this and any other world out of nothing (if God Wills it to be so).

Regardless of one's conclusion as to the degree to which God is dependent upon Its creation (whilst remaining outside of it) it becomes abundantly clear that as soon as we separate "God" from the "world" we run into exponential degrees of increasing complexity. The difficulty with panentheism is that it requires increasingly complicated (if not convoluted) philosophical rationales (or simply blind faith) in order to sustain it without inconsistencies. The more you separate God from creation, the more contradiction you encounter. It is this attempt at separating the material from the spiritual – the outer world from its inner creative Life Force – which brings ambiguity and paradox to the search for truth.

Pantheism does not require such mental gymnastics. It simply states that the world is God, everything is One, and leaves to the participants of that creation the task of uncovering how it works – and many have.

In fact, so many throughout history have uncovered this simple truth within their own experience that few, if any, obstacles remain for it to dawn upon the minds of even the most obstinate inquirers. Today, leading-edge investigators in science have now taken to exploring the world in terms of nonduality, quantum unity, wholistic entanglement, harmonics and resonance, collective consciousness, hive systems, sharing economies, sacred geometry and more. All of these approaches begin or end with the fundamental understanding that the world is nondual (One) and that nature, God and humankind are all varying aspects of the same existence.

Despite the 'user-friendliness' of nonduality and pantheism, the last several thousand years have seen whole societies and their systems (including mainstream religion, economics, law and even science) constructed on a worldview espousing quite the opposite – a worldview based on separateness, fragmentation, difference, individualism and privileged hierarchy. In the meantime, nondualism and unitive systems of thinking have been systematically demoted to the categories of wishful thinking, blind faith, religiosity and metaphysical mumbo-jumbo. While the materialistic and reductionist worldview has been useful for classifying the objective material appearance of the world, it has necessarily led to a deep and unrelenting manifestation of alienation, isolation, scarcity, subversion, oppression, enslavement and chaos. Not only has this material dualism established a type of existential alienation between members of the human family but has led to the prevailing experience of estrangement from both the observed world around us (i.e. nature) as well as the unseen world (i.e. God). This disaffecting approach has created a vast emotional desert, giving rise to countless numbers of "isms" in order to fill the void left by this dislocation and with each new belief system acting as its own barrier to the search for meaning. Each "ism" stands in as an inferior replacement for what should be a conscious *livingness* 'in the moment' which can engender a sense of purpose, meaning and place in the universe.

The mind and its many ideas and beliefs can generate a very definite prison for the individual whose walls – built of the energies of *thought* and fortified by the crystallising forces of uncompromising *ideas* and *ideology* – further obscure and condition the experiences which the indwelling consciousness could have as it peers *through* those 'isms' at the world. An individual's identity, constructed as it is of past experience and further enshrined in present beliefs and ideas constitutes the 'ring pass not' or boundary within which the 'psychological inmate' unwittingly reinforces his or her own sense of isolation and alienation.

On this point, it is valuable to emphasise that it is the willful *identification* with one idea or another, one 'ism' or another, which makes possible the imprisonment of the consciousness more than do the actual contents of any particular belief or view. It is not the idea itself which presents the fundamental problem for the individual nor the clarity or comprehension that the individual may have about that idea. It is not even significant whether the concept is rational or accurate. A fundamentalist of a particular viewpoint remains hopelessly chained to their beliefs because of their fierce *identification* with that particular notion. It is this identification with the idea which constitutes the blinding force for an individual through which even logic, facts and common sense are difficult to penetrate.

Societies and whole cultures have been built upon the foundation stones of 'isms'. Whether political, religious or economic, these ideas have provided the pillars upon which the personal identities of billions of Souls throughout history have been further formed. Chief amongst the multiplicity of ideas which have caused the most grief and suffering for humanity has been our identification with the notion that we are separate from one another, from nature and from the divine. Where this original and deep-seated dualism is paired with virtually any other secondary idea or ideal you will have the formation of war, opposition, division, destruction, polarisation or impasse. On the other hand, wherever a nondual attitude can provide the backdrop to other ideas and ideals then a natural empathy and rapport is created between disparate or opposing viewpoints. In fact, adopting a nondual understanding of the world is quite unique in that it acts both as an antidote to the internal generation of a 'separate self' as well as a sort of natural immunity against divisive ideologies or beliefs. Where one sees the world as One, war and conflict become irrational and untenable. Where a widespread *realisation* exists that the world is one, war and conflict become impossible.

There can be little wonder, therefore, that we find ourselves in a period of history steeped in fragmentation, discord, disenfranchisement, alienation and bigotry whilst, at the same time, living through one of the most self-centred and materialistically-minded centuries on record. A few of the most immediate expressions of this fragmentation can be seen in the elevation of the material lifestyle and worldview, widespread social hedonism, the advent of self-centered psychology, the primacy of personal wealth economics and the popularity of abundance-focused religion (abundance sought for oneself rather than for the basic needs of others). Catastrophically, when we are unable to mask or suppress the experience of suffering that arises as a result of this over-emphasis on individualism and individual pursuits then we turn to distraction or intoxication. Drugs, sex, sports, work and even the endless hum and buzz of mobile phones are employed to stand in for at least some semblance of connectedness – or at least to numb the sting of separation.

In our minds the world has become a cold and abandoning experience, devoid of fundamental meaning and purpose. In response to this alienation, we substitute in our own purpose – to raise a family, to buy a house, to get that promotion or raise, to be in relationship with someone – but it never quite brings lasting satisfaction where the underlying worldview reinforces the experience of separation and disconnection. A close examination of the motives behind our actions can often reveal the need of being accepted, of being loved and of the need for a sense of *belonging*. The irony in this tragedy is that we are *already* connected to one another and we only experience disunity as a result of the illusion created by our limited perception and understanding of the world. The more we attempt to seek security from the outer world, the more insecure and alone we become in our inner lives.

Science today is the result of an enormous effort and achievement by dedicated individuals on behalf of humanity and its progress. Our civilisation owes a great debt to those fellow travellers who have sought to penetrate the mysteries of our physical world. The vast potential offered to humanity through the inventions and discoveries of the last one hundred years is beyond calculation. However, much of what could have been achieved in the last three centuries remains squandered through the ill-effects of division, competition and self-centered pursuit. What science has uncovered in terms of technological wonder is often offset by its approach to life as a mechanical linear process. For all of its wondrous invention, science remains incapable of providing even a coherent or robust explanation for the principles of either 'consciousness' or 'life'. Were either of these to be captured or reproduced within the boundaries of the laboratory the fundamental problems for humanity could be overturned entirely. Unfortunately, hardly one substantial hypothesis has yet to be put forward from within the materialist's satchel that could bring us any nearer the desired target. It is only those few who have begun to reach beyond the proscribed tools of empirical investigation, and who have often paid the price of reputation and position, that are making meaningful strides today.

Interestingly, breakthroughs in recent decades have demonstrated just how interconnected and 'entangled' is the entire matrix of the cosmos. Pythagoras declared that "all things are number" and the recent resurrection of studies in sacred geometry and the function of Toroidal Force in nature suggests that we are on the doorstep of an entirely new understanding of ourselves and the universe. Advancements in quantum mechanics, alongside emerging evidence that consciousness itself plays an intricate and essential role in unfolding the evolutionary process makes it impossible to deny that our thoughts, beliefs and ideas are part of the fundamental mechanisms behind creation. "We are the world and the world is in us". While such a statement would typically be more at home in the Vedas or Upanishads it is now increasingly found in the pages of scientific journals and the halls of cutting-edge research. What is becoming rapidly clearer is that we are living in a profoundly interconnected universe, despite what appears to our limited material senses as a fragmented or chaotic world. It is becoming more and more undeniable that we live and operate under laws that govern unity rather than discontinuity, and we progress in our understanding according to our capacity to align ourselves with those principles of unity.

Recent research by Canadian ecologist Suzanne Simard revealed an example of how unified systems can operate within even the most common of natural systems. Simard's investigations have shown how trees communicate to one another using an underground network of soil fungi and bacteria. This system can transmit signals of the presence of unfolding threats – such as clear-cutting or climate change – to neighbouring trees and plants or can share nutrients and other resources to specific plants within the eco-system that may be experiencing hardship. From a September 01, 2016 interview in *Yale Environment 360*, published by the Yale School of Forestry and Environmental Studies, Simard described this unified network and its function:

> It's this network, sort of like a below-ground pipeline, that connects one tree root system to another tree root system, so that nutrients and carbon and water can exchange between the trees. In a natural forest of British Columbia, paper birch and Douglas fir grow together in early successional forest communities. They compete with each other, but our work shows that they also cooperate with each other by sending nutrients and carbon back and forth through their mycorrhizal (fungi) networks...
>
> One of the important things that we tested in that particular experiment was shading. The more Douglas fir became shaded in the summertime, the more excess carbon the birch had went to the fir. Then later in the fall, when the birch was losing its leaves and the fir had excess carbon because it was still photosynthesizing, the net transfer of this exchange went back to the birch.

Incredible as it sounds to have entire ecological systems sharing resources, Simard goes on to describe the work of research student Kevin Bailer who analysed DNA samples in patches of Douglas fir tree forests. He was able to create a map showing the interrelation of all the trees and how they were linked together.

> He found that the biggest, oldest trees in the network were the most highly linked, whereas smaller trees were not linked to as many other trees. Big old trees have got bigger root systems and associate with bigger mycorrhizal networks...
> In later experiments, we've been pursuing whether these older trees can recognize kin, whether the seedlings that are regenerating around them are the same kin, whether they're offspring or not, and whether they can favour those seedlings - and we found that they can. That's how we came up with the term "mother tree", because they're the biggest, oldest trees, and we know that they can nurture their own kin.

While the work by Simard and others continues, and generates its own share of sceptics as to whether this can actually be called some form of 'communication' between plant species, it is abundantly clear that we live in a world deeply interconnected and that this unity is beginning to reveal itself in a variety of unexpected fields. It is little wonder that the holy grail of cosmological study today is to develop a 'theory of everything' – some ultimate or all-encompassing coherent framework to explain and link together modern physics (general relativity) and quantum field theory. That this movement in thought even posits the possibility of one fundamental theory to explain everything shows just how intuitively satisfying the idea of unity has become.

The great Indian sage Nagarjuna lived in northern India during the second century. His arrival was foretold over 500 years earlier by Gautama Buddha who prophesied that his teachings on the dharma and suffering would one day fall to distortion and misinterpretation, and that a disciple of the Naga (serpent wisdom) sect would come forth to restore the true meaning of the teachings. Nagarjuna's teachings stand to this day as one of the definitive works of logic on nonduality, as well as the incoherence and irrationality of holding a dualistic materialist worldview.

Nagarjuna introduced the notion of the Two Truths. The first Truth is known as the 'conventional world' which we all experience through the senses and which we generally accept to be 'basic reality'. This reality appears to us as a dualistic, separate and material reality – a world comprised of apparent subjects and object. It is the world that our consciousness perceives through the filter of the five material senses (taste, touch, scent, sound and sight). It is through this sensory experience that consciousness is conditioned to think of itself as a separate entity in relationship to other objects and entities in the material universe. The experience of separativeness is so overwhelming, prevailing and comprehensive that it is extremely difficult for consciousness to formulate any other version of reality. Even when, in rare moments, it might touch beyond that boundary it is seldom able to interpret that subjective experience in any manner than through dualistic words or concepts. Thus lays the challenge for consciousness as it evolves its own expression and self-perception through these lower material planes of reality.

Nagarjuna's second Truth is described fittingly as *"reality-as-it-is"*, the Absolute or the Logos. It is 'Buddha-Mind', unfragmented, whole, complete and unbroken in its entirety. It is the state of cosmos as it is, before the activity of mind applies its differentiating and naming activity. It exists at all moments, throughout the universe, and is entirely whole in all its Beingness. It can be described inadequately by many names and forms yet, in and of itself, remains nameless and formless. It cannot truly be described, but can only be 'Known' when all thinking, naming and 'personal intention' has been quieted.

For Christians, the "Christ in you" which leads to knowledge that the "Kingdom of Heaven is in you and all around". This notion runs entirely parallel to the Buddhist's search for "Buddha-mind in all things" and its capacity to produce "liberation from the travails of samsara [illusion], ending in nirvana [liberation from illusion]". By whatever name is put to that all-pervading unconditioned consciousness, it has the capacity to penetrate the great illusion of Forms (including 'thoughts' as part of the world of forms). This unconditioned consciousness reveals to us that there is no "there" in terms of heaven, satori, fana, nirvana or any other term used to describe that state of awareness which is enlightenment or liberation beyond death. As Nagarjuna would reveal, both samsara and nirvana (alongside the ideas of heaven and hell for Christians) are simply notions, concepts or thoughtforms created by the thought-making processes of the mind and it is only by going beyond "thinking" and the making of "ideas about the world" that consciousness can finally experience the true 'nirvana-like' or 'heaven-like' unconditioned and whole reality – *reality-as-it-is*.

We are confronted with an all-embracing, yet simple, realisation. Consciousness, while immersed in the experience of material reality, seeks to know and understand itself in that experience. However, it is unable to fully perceive itself or reality-as-it-is through the limitations of the material senses. It constructs an individual persona for itself by identifying itself with the ideas, beliefs, sensations, perceptions and relationships that it comes to accumulate from its environment. The illusion of 'separateness' is created, leading to the ongoing experience of disconnection, alienation and suffering. As the 12th century neo-Confucian philosopher Lu Hsiang-shan said, "The Universe has never separated itself from man. Man separates himself from the Universe". It is the suffering from this separation which provides the stimulus to seek a deeper understanding of life and its laws, and that advances the pilgrim toward a greater self-awareness of their true divine nature and eventual liberation. For Nagarjuna, this separation is unreal and temporary. However, through its identification with conventional truth, consciousness becomes mired in this illusion along with the consequent suffering born of separation.

    A vast anthology of philosophical and spiritual writings exists in both Eastern and Western traditions which describe the nature of reality as 'nondual' or fundamentally 'One'. I have also described how consciousness, experiencing reality *through* the filters of the material senses, misinterprets reality in terms of subject-object relations (dualism). Consciousness, which is part of the Whole, experiences itself as a disconnected fragment in the material world. There is no way for us to know the "purpose" of the Absolute (God). One might reason, however, that the manifestation of God's purpose would necessarily be in the form of an expression of complete wholeness, synthesis and unity on all planes of existence. That is, if the nature of reality-as-it-is resembles oneness then the ultimate purpose for the Absolute could only be expressed in the form of a completely synthesised Unity. Moreover, if humanity is some aspect or appearance of that Absolute (like the waves on the ocean) then whatever ultimate purpose there might be in store for humanity must also be manifested and expressed as that completely synthesised Unity. This is an important point which warrants serious consideration.

Notwithstanding this inference, I would like to set aside any further conjecture on the idea of God's "purpose" since, at this stage in our evolution, that can serve to create another 'idea' for our illusory personal identity. We can reason that when the capacity is achieved by humanity to recognise its purpose in the Universe then that resolution must necessarily manifest itself as a demonstration in unconditional and total Unity. Furthermore, it may only be by the manifestation of that Unity through which humanity's purpose may eventually become known. It is only by working toward the achievement of unity in every avenue of society and every aspect of our civilisation that we might finally demonstrate that full nature of who we are and be in a position to express that unified principle on behalf of the divine nature of the Universe.

The Origins of Separation

> The body is mortal, but he who dwells in the body is immortal and immeasurable.
>
> – *The Bhagavad Gita*

The notion of some original separation by humanity from the 'One' or the 'Whole' is found throughout almost all major spiritual traditions. While the reason for this separation is somewhat varied – due largely to the diverse perspectives, cultures and languages involved – it is interesting to note that every scheme begins with unity, moves through a period of disunity and suffering, and then returns once again along a Path or Way of redemption to a state of unity (or, more accurately, liberation from the illusion of disunity). That this return to unity is somewhat of a universal story provides hope for the future and brings purpose to our daily struggles. These stories (described by some as "myths" and "legends") present a common narrative wherein humanity, at some 'beginning' time, underwent a separation or 'fall' from its original state of union with its divine source. Whether one describes that source as the Absolute, God, Brahman, the Universal, the Divine, the Whole or some other original state of existence, there unfolded some evolutionary

The Origins of Separation

event which resulted in the 'descending' or immersion of divine consciousness into matter and material forms. It was this *involution* into matter and form where our perceptions of oneness with the divine became obscured and lost. It is significant to remember that actual unity with the divine is never, and could never, be lost and it is only the *perception* of unity which becomes distorted. It is this expedition into the material form life from which the 'prodigal son' must eventually return to his father.

Most accounts begin with a certain state of original union with God which becomes distorted through the first appearance of 'mind' with its discriminatory powers and rudimentary self-awareness. This is the achievement – in itself an evolutionary coup – which also obscured the earlier perceptions of unity. This initial 'dividing oneself out from the whole' immediately gives rise to the symbolic 'rebellion' against the state of divinity and divine unity. This rebellion by humanity – the 'fallen angel' – also results in the emergence of characteristics previously unknown such as selfishness and mortality. At the heart of it, these stories are really speaking about "beings of consciousness" becoming "beings of consciousness in material form".

In many African societies, a variety of myths describe how, in primordial times, this original separation between man and

God came about. The BaSonge tradition of Zaire describes the event in this way:

> The Creator, Fidi Mukullu, made all things including man. He also planted banana trees. When the bananas were ripe He sent the sun to harvest them. The sun brought back a full basket to Fidi Mukullu, who asked him if he had eaten any. The sun answered "no," and the Creator decided to put him to a test. He made the sun go down into a hole dug in the earth, then asked him when he wanted to get out. "Tomorrow morning, early," answered the sun. "If you did not lie," the Creator told him, "you will get out early tomorrow morning." The next day the sun appeared at the desired moment, confirming his honesty. Next the moon was ordered to gather God's bananas and was put to the same test. She also got out successfully. Then came man's turn to perform the same task. However, on his way to the Creator he ate a portion of the bananas, but denied doing so. Put to the same test as the sun and the moon, man said that he wanted to leave the hole at the end of five days. But he never got out. Fidi Mukullu said, "Man lied. That is why man will die and will never reappear."

In Burundi, the Urundi tribe speak of how an encounter with death and attempted deception introduced mortality to the human family.

> In the olden days, when God still lived among men, Death did not live among men. Whenever he happened to stray onto the earth, God (Imana) would chase it away with his hunting dogs. One day during such a chase, Death was forced into a narrow space and would have been caught and destroyed. But in his straits he found a woman, and promised her that if she hid him he would spare her and her family. The woman opened her mouth and Death jumped inside. When God came to her and asked her if she had seen Death, she denied ever seeing him. But God, the All-Seeing One, knew what happened, and told the woman that since she had hidden Death, in the future Death would destroy her and all her children. From that moment death spread all over the world.

The Dinka of Sudan spoke of an original union between God and man which only becomes interrupted when greed arose.

> In the beginning God was very close to man, for the sky then lay just above the earth. There was no death, sickness, sorrow, or hunger, and men were content with one grain of millet a day granted them by God. One day, a greedy woman,

who wanted to pound more than the one grain permitted, used a long-handled pestle and struck the sky. This angered God, who withdrew with the sky to its present position far above the earth. Since then the country has become spoiled, and men are now subject to death, sickness, hunger, and disease.

The Abrahamic traditions (Judaism, Christianity and Islam) share this common doctrine of an original Fall from a primordial state of unity with God. In many ways, the previous African narratives mirror the fate which befalls Adam and Eve in the Genesis story – although the purpose for the Fall is interpreted somewhat variously between the Abrahamic faiths.

In Christianity, partaking of fruit from the tree of knowledge – and specifically the knowledge of 'good and evil' (i.e., duality) – creates an enduring separation between humanity and God, along with a subsequent expulsion from Paradise or Eden. This is the 'original sin' of Christian doctrine which finds its eventual resolution in, or through, the historical Christ.

Islam adopts a basically similar interpretation of the Fall but, instead of redemption through Christ, humanity can return to a state of acceptance and unity in paradise through submission to God. Judaism provides yet another variance to this story, and the sin of Adam and Eve

The Origins of Separation

which led to the Fall is incorporated as part of the original intention or plan of God. In this way humanity is responsible for its own fall from unity with God yet, by doing so, is also fulfilling the larger plan of God. Needless to say, the undeniable theme within all of these accounts accepts the existence of an original unity between humanity and the Divine, a subsequent engagement with the perspectives of dualism and materiality, and a separation (intended or unintended) from the state of Eden-like unity. This Fall leads to all the negative attributes and characteristics that can only arise in this state of separation. It is in this new state of identification with the material world that humanity encounters physical disease, hunger, alienation, discord and the experience of mortality and death.

An interesting side note might be of concern to the reader as it pertains to a specific reference in the Abrahamic doctrine. I have often reflected on the notion that Man (meaning humankind as a whole, of course) was "made in the image of God". Let us presume for the sake of simplicity that "Man" in this instance is represented by 'Adam and Eve' and whatever literal or symbolic portrayal that represents. It is also important that we understand that the occasion of the original creation of Adam and Eve occurred *before* the Fall. This is significant, and lends further to the premise that I have tried to establish in this treatise. If Adam and Eve were created in the image of God, and that 'image' is one which existed before the Fall, then this statement would not be referring to that later state of *material* form which Adam and Eve entered into *after* the Fall. It is not the physical form of a male or a female which merits this reference to the image of God but it is to that pre-Fall state where consciousness is still a 'consciousness in union with the Divine'. In that sense, there is no particular 'form' that we can ascribe to humanity at that stage other than simply a 'divine state of Being'. Perhaps some reflection on the notion of this unified pre-Fall state of Being might help to adjust our thinking about who we are. It might even give a hint at some further aspect of God.

Eastern religious and philosophical traditions do not offer a similar illustrative story of the Fall as does the Abrahamic traditions but, nevertheless, include within their doctrines a consistent description of the *condition* of humanity which somewhat parallels its western siblings. The true spiritual nature of humanity is described as veiled within the shroud of material identification. This deviation in self-awareness arises from the presence of impurities and illusions which distort reality. All is Atma, and no truly independent 'self' exists outside of Brahman, the Absolute. The separate individual 'self' – the 'little personal self' – is an illusory construct which can be overcome eventually through the practice of exercises or devotions which can liberate the inner consciousness from this illusion. In this sense, eastern traditions align much more readily with the esoteric and mystery traditions. Steeped in allegory and metaphor, Buddhism, Jainism and many other Eastern traditions describe a gradual decline from an earlier Godlike state into a degenerate state of vice and license. Through eons of the misuse of human nature, mankind has brought itself to a state of depravity requiring periodic intervention and reorientation onto the path leading to salvation and eventual enlightenment. The goal for humanity is the path of purification proceeding step by step to full Self-realisation (as one with the Divine). One's own nature is the Divine Atma, which is also part of the Divine Whole or the Absolute. This journey, from Wholeness to degeneration and back to Perfection, is a great play in the Mind of Cosmos or Brahma.

In these short descriptions we can again see the process of unity-disunity-suffering-rehabilitation-reunion emerge. Impurity and misunderstanding, while immersed in material existence, are factors lying behind the original loss of conscious unity with the creator. The disciple must thereafter undergo any number of purifications or rehabilitative exercises that are designed to eventually clear the 'inner sight' and lead to the liberation of consciousness from illusion. This liberation is the return to a state of unity with the Divine. The original descent from perfection is described for us in the Hindu tradition from the Mahabharata:

> Formerly Prajapati brought forth pure creatures, were truthful and virtuous. These creatures joined the gods in the sky whenever they wished, and they lived and died by their own wish. In another time, those who dwelt on earth were overcome by desire and anger, and they were abandoned by the gods. Then by their foul deeds these evil ones were trapped in the chain of rebirth, and they became atheists [no longer 'knowers of the gods'].

In this passage we are reacquainted with the idea that it was the immersion of human consciousness into earthly matter and form that had the effect of 'trapping' or 'chaining' humankind to the circumstances of death and rebirth in the material world. Once 'involved' with matter, the interaction of consciousness with this 'less pure' material corrupts its activity and experience. The Soul is trapped, and its expression in the world through matter becomes distorted by the imperfections in that material world.

For Taoists, the writings in the Tao Te Ching describe this same descent for consciousness into corruption.

> When the Tao was lost, there was virtue;

> When virtue was lost, there was benevolence;
> When benevolence was lost, there was rectitude;
> When rectitude was lost, there were rules of propriety
> Propriety is a wearing thin of loyalty and good faith,
> And the beginning of disorder.

Such is the manner by which consciousness progressively descends in character to become trapped and imprisoned in matter. As the higher consciousness becomes increasingly enthralled by matter its subsequent identification with the material vehicle and its imperfections hinder the expression of the Soul's virtues on the physical plane. The degree to which this identification with matter occurs determines, among other things, how much of the Soul's selfless nature – or the personal identity's selfish nature – can be expressed.

In the Dhammapada, the Buddha spoke of a high state of achievement wherein the disciple can find eventual rehabilitation and release. The challenge for the indwelling consciousness or Soul (the 'Self') is to discipline and tame its vehicles of manifestation (the 'little self' or individual personality) and to elevate them cnough to once again be a pure channel for the Soul.

The monk is said to be a Bhikkhu of peace when his body, words and mind are peaceful, when he is master of himself and when he has left behind the lower attractions of the world.

Arise! Rouse thyself by thy Self; train thyself by thy Self. Under the shelter of thy Self, and ever watchful, thou shalt live in supreme joy.

For thy Self is the master of thyself, and thy Self is thy refuge. Train therefore thyself well, even as a merchant trains a fine horse.

To conquer the imperfections of one's lower vehicles and to overcome the pull of the lower material nature is the challenge set forth for the man or woman if they are to overcome their imprisonment in form. "If a man should conquer in battle a thousand and a thousand more", said the Buddha, "and another man should conquer himself, his would be the greater victory, because the greatest of victories is the victory over oneself". Most notably is that stage of complete self-awareness wherein the indwelling consciousness can find eventual release and liberation from the grip of dualism and materiality. The final and most difficult realisation of the Self is in knowing that it is not only distinct from the physical, emotional and mental vehicles it has built but is also one with That which is called the Absolute. In this achievement the Self is released from bondage in the material world. Once again from the Dhammapada,

> O builder of the house, now you are seen.
> You will not build the house again.
> All your rafters are broken, your ridge-pole is destroyed.
> Your mind has attained the extinction of desires.
> It is set on the attainment of Nirvana.

When the Self can finally achieve an awareness and understanding of itself as the consciousness which stands behind the creation of all its vehicles of manifestation it can then stand free of the identifications and personas (rafters and ridge-poles) in which it had unwittingly veiled itself. In this manner we see the cycle completed and, as we saw similarly in previous traditions, humanity undergoes a process of separation, further struggle and suffering in that state of disunity. This suffering eventually prompts the effort to return and reunite with the Whole. Thus flows the breath of the Divine, first pouring itself out into the material world, experiencing all that is possible for consciousness to know, and then returning to its source once again – fillcd with knowledge of itself in every form and quality, every characteristic and feature possible. In this great movement, the Divine comes to

Know and Manifest Itself throughout Creation.

It is worth emphasising a point which should now be growing in the mind of the reader. While I have attempted to form an image of the process which consciousness undergoes on its journey from unity to separation and back to unity again, it is important to understand that this process exists only in the perceptions received by the Self and no true or ultimate separation ever occurs. It is the *illusion* of separation which overtakes the understanding held by the indwelling Soul as it perceives the world through its material vehicles and then identifies with that distorted observation. But no *actual* separation can be said to have occurred – for only 'the Whole' exists at any moment. There is no separate location or position that is outside of the Whole. The conviction which arises regarding separation or being 'other than' the objects in your surroundings arises entirely as a result of how our senses frame and filter reality for us.

An experience of how this works can be somewhat illustrated through a simple mental exercise in which the reader can engage. Currently, you are reading these words and participating in a thought exercise to observe your present experience. As you read, you are also experiencing yourself looking out at the page and perhaps trying to relate these ideas to your own understanding of who or what you are. Without even having to think the thoughts, you 'understand' yourself to be an individual person separate and apart from the book and its pages. Alas, this first basic deduction is *wrong* and constitutes the first fundamental illusion generated by the senses and long-held mental construct of yourself. Moreover, despite this illusion being exposed to you in this very moment it remains nearly impossible to see it otherwise since your consciousness, which comprehends these words, has identified itself so fundamentally and extensively with the 'idea' of the persona which you accept to be 'you' – built, as it is, with the rafters and ridge-poles of thoughts and beliefs about 'yourself'. What you may now be experiencing by this phase in the exercise is just how all-encompassing and how deeply that conviction is that your consciousness is submerged in its identity. This is not to say that everything you believe your 'self' to be – your name, your gender, your relationships, likes and dislikes – is an illusion, but these all belong to the vehicle that you have created. It is not the consciousness which is, itself, looking at the pages of the book *through* the vehicle you have constructed. Try to step back from your identity and imagine, just for a moment, that the only real thing is this consciousness which is perceiving. Let go of the whole complex of thoughts, feelings, emotions and sensations and try to isolate in your experience only that which is consciousness, the observer, free of thoughts in the moment. Do not judge or analyse this consciousness, but simply 'be' it, if only for an instant, free of the edifice it has taken a lifetime to build. Step back entirely within yourself, and only focus on the 'experiencing' aspect of yourself. You are *only* this observer, and the rest is illusion. If you are able to enter this experience momentarily, not through creating an idea of it but by removing all ideas and identifications, you will be touching the first fringes of that inner being which is called the Divine Self. In that moment, as you have been reading, you will feel no sense of separation, loneliness or suffering. It is a space of wholeness. Alternatively, where even the slightest hint of emotions, memories or thoughts surface back into your experience you can be sure that the separate 'identity' has crept back onto the stage and re-asserted its dominance over your experience.

This exercise can help to create a starting point for the individual upon which to build further experiences of disentanglement. Even if the previous exercise did not yield a full measure of detachment from the identity the mere attempt can help to render an appreciation for the possibility of one day standing free of one or another of the self-created illusory vehicles. The evolution of consciousness demands that a fuller self-awareness continues to unfold while still immersed in the material world. However, the achievements of true detachment and eventual liberation are evidenced when the consciousness begins to know itself as 'real' and independent of its manifestations. This realisation can begin to demonstrate as an increasingly conscious mastery over its vehicles. When this has been fully achieved the Soul is nearing the path of liberation and the complete cessation of suffering.

The celebrated sage and spiritual teacher Ramana Maharshi provided a more direct and penetrating account on discovering that Self which lies behind the manufactured persona. In *Self Inquiry* and *Who Am I*, Ramana Maharshi deconstructs the illusion which is the superficial identity and helps the reader to seek the true Self within. Starting with the inquiry "who am I", and eliminating those layers of identity which were believed to be oneself, Maharshi asserts that one's essential nature can be discovered. From *The Collected Works of Ramana Maharshi*, we read,

> For obtaining such knowledge the inquiry 'Who am I?' in quest of Self is the best means...
> Therefore, summarily rejecting all the above-mentioned physical adjuncts and their functions, saying 'I am not this; no, nor am I this, nor this' – that which then remains separate and alone by itself, that pure Awareness is what I am...
> If in this manner the mind becomes absorbed in the Heart, the ego or 'I'...

finally vanishes and pure Consciousness or Self, which subsists during all the states of mind, alone resplendent.

What has been emphasised by spiritual teachers throughout the ages is this fact of both the existence and non-existence of separation. Where consciousness has identified itself with the separate vehicle it has created separation through the notion of 'I' arising alongside the illusion that "I am different or separate from you". Where consciousness can step back from that notion of 'I', a realisation occurs that separation never existed in reality but only made its appearance within that mental framework of 'I'.

Nagarjuna set out his system of reasoning and demonstrated quite logically that dualism and the existence of 'separateness', despite being the way that we perceive the world, cannot rationally be defended as real. Moreover, logic further dictates that reality must be nondual or Whole. However, the problem for the enquirer is that you can't make the claim that reality is nondual since such a claim is in the realm of thoughts and beliefs and, therefore, the creation of a thoughtform about it is simply another form of making it part of duality. You can directly experience nondual reality-as-it-is (i.e., nirvana, heaven, etc) *but if you start to create any thoughts or ideas about it* then you are creating a second-hand illusory form in the mind. You turn nondual reality into a duality.

This revealing deduction by Nagarjuna pinpoints the problem facing the seeker and also accounts for the existence of the paradox or contraction that arises in many spiritual teachings. Reality *does* exist as a nondual 'whole'. However, to speak or think about it in any 'form' reduces it to an unreal illusion in the realm of subjects and objects. Therefore, it cannot ultimately be described or discussed – it can only be experienced directly. This accounts for why the Buddha never spoke about 'God' or the individual 'Soul' other than to assert that they did not exist. Any conversation that He could have had about them would be an exercise in upholding illusion. Like our earlier thought experiment, we can strip away the various layers of identity until only the experience of consciousness and unadulterated awareness remains – the presence of Being or livingness in the moment. Consciousness, in this sense, cannot be further 'described' because to do so is to reduce it to the realm of thoughts and ideas and to make of it just another facet of the construct of 'I'. This notion allowed Nagarjuna to declare that "samsara is nirvana, and nirvana is samsara". Both the world of illusion (dualistic samsara) and the world of liberation (nondualistic nirvana) are unreal where they are discussed as mere ideas within which identity can become further embroiled.

It is not difficult to see this same idea described by the Christ in the instruction to His disciples, "the kingdom of heaven is in you and all around you" and that an experience of that state could be known to everyone through "the Christ in you [the Christ consciousness], the hope and glory". The Katha Upanishad repeats this idea of penetrating the chrysalis of personal identity and the thoughtforms we create about ourselves in order to find the divine consciousness within and the Oneness with all that exists.

> Finer than the finest, larger than the largest, is the Self (atman) that lies here hidden in the heart of a living being. Without desires and free from sorrow, a man perceives by the creator's grace the grandeur of the Self.

This discussion can have some implications for how the reader may approach the interpretation of various sacred writings and scriptures, and suggests the possibility of creating a more synthetic understanding between eastern and western doctrines. For example, if we can momentarily suspend our traditional interpretations of many western scriptures (for 'interpretation' is all that really exists) we might reveal something of previously unrealised meaning. The distinct possibility arises that eastern and western cultures were not as isolated from one another – either geographically or philosophically – as our historical records may sometimes want to suggest. It is quite possible that philosophical and spiritual ideas freely flowed between eastern and western cultures as well as from the north and south.

It is here that the teachings of Esoteric Philosophy provide another perspective not often contemplated within the halls of contemporary mainstream religion. The Ageless Wisdom Teachings (also known as Esoteric Philosophy) have put forward methods and means whereby such an inner unity with the Divine might be undertaken. These formerly hidden or obscure traditions will reach more prominence and relevance in the coming time as the realisation unfolds that humanity is in the process of unfolding a fuller expression of the Divine from within themselves. Mystery traditions have often explored the evolution and struggle of consciousness from the perspective of its imprisonment in, and subsequent liberation from, the material world. The Soul, described also in various traditions as the "Christ Consciousness" or the "Christ in you" discovers itself for the first time in the Garden of Eden. It is the initial awareness of consciousness of its material vehicle, and identification with matter and the material form, which is the separative factor that sets in motion the long journey of suffering.

The esoteric tradition states that the only real 'sin' is the sin of separation. It was that original dualistic perspective of 'good' and 'evil' (subject-object), developed during the early descent of humanity's consciousness into material form, which resulted in the perceived loss of unity with the Divine. It is the struggle of consciousness to know itself beyond its material identification which will bring consciousness back to a state of unity with its own true nature – the Divine. The experience of identification with the material forms generates the friction and fires of the evolutionary impulse to grow. This impulse to know one's Self carries the consciousness onward to seek its own true nature. And it is through the discovery of the 'Christ [consciousness] within' every individual that the Soul can come to know itself and bring suffering to an end.

What is just as important as the story of "how we got here" from that original state of unity is to ask "how do we get back"? The more common accounts appear to include some period of penance and suffering to be endured by humanity after which certain rehabilitative and redemptive pursuits will lead humanity, individually, to reunification with the Divine. Setting aside for a moment the various how's and whereby's of that redemptive path there is no disagreement among the various faiths that the ultimate goal is to achieve some eventual reunion with God. History and the theologians of all persuasions have largely laid emphasis on the erring ways of humanity alongside a prescription for punishment and atonement. Perhaps our present collective readiness for understanding the importance of unity might signal the need to shift our emphasis onto the many ways which can manifest that reunification and unity in our lives.

One final observation arises out of this last revelatory notion. Humanity has, for millennia, waited in anticipation for a 'saviour' – some divine personage who is expected to lift the burden of separation from the shoulders of loyal or devoted followers and reunite them with their Creator. Psychologists might suggest that this hope is really a projection onto some outer figure of an essential inner process. If the thesis I have explored here is closer to the truth then *the Saviour has been here with us all along, and lives within the Heart of every human being.* That 'saving' opportunity remains hidden in plain view and is the Light of Consciousness itself. No outside personality could ever fulfil such a role for another and no mystic, sage or true spiritual teacher will ever infringe on the discovery of that ultimate teacher within – since it is that discovery of the Self by the little 'self' which seems to be the entire goal of evolution. Waiting to be 'saved' by some outer material figure is surely the interim expectation prior to discovering the true saving quality of the divine consciousness within.

The view presented in this chapter can be applied equally across a variety of traditions without the need to change the texts themselves or alter the words. It will transform the interpreted meaning of those texts and words and unite them in a common outlook and perspective. This perspective has the power to turn any doctrine into a personal *living* experience rather than an impersonal dogma or codex of rules and behaviours. It is my fervent belief that any teaching worthy of its teacher was meant to be a living, breathing experience for its adherents. Such a quality has within it the breath of the Ageless Wisdom and, hopefully, such a quality has been passed onto the reader through these thoughts on unity.

The Illusion of Separation

> What need is there of any vows save
> the vow to guard the thoughts?
>
> – *Shantideva*

An effort would not be wasted here if we took a moment to explore the idea of illusion and how the world around us can be interpreted as something other than what it is. I am confident that an extensive treatise will one day be written on the myriad of distorting influences and factors that could stand between reality-as-it-is and consciousness as it attempts to make sense of its observations and perceptions. Philosophers have engaged in defining the contents of "reality" for millennia and will continue to do so for millennia to come. I would like to present some of my own thoughts to that inquiry in hopes that it might provide additional insights to a problem which afflicts every human being. It is hoped that this addition can help to further the reader's own examination into what is often a confusing and obtuse topic.

The problem of illusion confronts us every day and in many ways. We look out upon the world and, for the most part, we fit together a snapshot of the world which, at first blush, is visually similar to what any other person registers. We share the same physical senses. For the most part we all participate by default in Nagarjuna's "conventional truth" about the events unfolding before us – whether that be the World Cup football game on television, spending an afternoon together with friends at the beach or reading the words of an article in a newspaper. Regardless of our positive or negative opinion about the unfolding events – and notwithstanding any deficiency in our individual sensory equipment – we share a common view of the world around us.

Following on the heels of this collective observation is the addition of our own individual interpretation and understanding of experience and it is predominantly at this stage where convention and agreement appear to break down. How is it that several individuals can witness the same event yet render entirely diverse, and even contradictory, interpretations? Two bystanders to an automobile accident can describe similar details yet completely dissimilar interpretations of the cause. One may describe a victim as confused while another may testify that the same victim was aloof or even the aggressor. How can such a divergence in opinion occur? Where does the Truth stand?

It is generally acknowledged in esoteric traditions that human consciousness is faced with the phenomenon of illusion in three major vehicles of expression: physical, emotional and mental. That is, when consciousness can overcome illusion as it functions on these three planes of perception then the capacity to gain control and mastery over the corresponding vehicles of expression becomes possible. Another way of describing this is that the individual is acquiring the capacity to liberate themselves from imprisonment on these planes of manifestation. Therefore, it is important to examine each of these aspects independent of one another in order to more clearly isolate and identify their influence in our own individual interpretations of reality. Simply seeing the effects of each of these on our perceptions can become the basis for overcoming its influence in our lives. This opportunity to examine our own inner workings can truly lead to inner transformation and the overcoming of those factors which lead to suffering.

Much progress has been made in understanding illusion on the physical plane due to the incredible advances in both science and spirituality over the last century and a half. Despite its tendency toward a materialistic interpretation of reality, scientific inquiry has penetrated beyond the mere 'forms' of our physical world to reveal an ocean of energetic waves that interrelate and interact at every mathematical point of space. Could we but truly see it, the universe would appear as an ocean of energy pulsating with life in every instance of space. Our consciousness operating through our five senses largely registers these energies as *forms* wherever the waves enhance or interfere with one another. The various forms which are created give us our 'picture' of the *physical* world, albeit far from being a total representation of the actual world. It is a picture which is fairly coherent across the broad spectrum of human sensory experience since we all share a commonly functioning physical body with physical senses. As our consciousness inhabits a physical form it identifies with that physical form and incorporates that appearance as constituting an actual representation of its Being.

This first form of illusion is referred to as *maya* in the eastern traditions and represents the initial layers of illusion through which consciousness must traverse on its way to liberation. That science has now penetrated that illusion through such fields as quantum mechanics and wholistic medicine is itself miraculous given that the illusion can only be seen beyond the senses. Nevertheless, it can be made to reveal itself to us through the design of experiments that uncover the behaviours of energies prior to appearing as 'form'. The result is the beginning of an understanding that our physical forms, our bodies of manifestation, are merely energetic structures held in place by the indwelling consciousness to establish a vehicle of expression for itself on the

The Illusion of Separation

physical plane. Likewise, where the indwelling consciousness identifies itself with this physical form so, too, does it become subject to the limitations in perception that this dense vehicle permits. Thus begins the early stages of suffering wherein the consciousness believes itself to be this separate and mortally vulnerable physical body.

Eastern traditions have described the nature of this illusion and its effects on consciousness for millennia and have produced volumes of instruction on the effects of its conditioning on the individual mind as well as methods leading to its overcoming. Training on detachment from the imprisoning hold of the senses on the mind is replete throughout the eastern doctrines and has found its way, in recent centuries, into many western spiritual movements. The steps to knowing the true inner self involve seeing that the physical body and the physical form are not the true self – is not the consciousness, nor the source of consciousness, in the person – but merely the chariot through which the consciousness experiences the physical world. According to the Buddha,

> The instructed disciple considers of the material shape, the other elements: 'This is not mine, I am not this, this is not my self'. So that when these elements change or become different he has no grief, or

sorrow, or suffering, or lamentation, or despair.

An important distinction is warranted here with regard to the notion of illusion in eastern traditions, and especially with how it is sometimes taught to those new to this idea. The notion is occasionally presented that "all reality is an illusion" and that, as such, unfolding events and circumstances contain no real meaning or consequence. This has particularly become popular amongst several spiritual or 'new age' movements in the west. Such a view is naïve and, in some cases, even dangerous. It should never be assumed that physical forms or physical events are illusory in the sense that they are not operating in the present moment. The physical world is not illusory in the sense that it does not exist. It is illusory in the sense that it is not a true identity of the indwelling consciousness. The physical vehicle, while not a principle for consciousness itself, remains an instrument of activity on the physical plane upon which the consciousness remains dependent for contact with the physical world. A very real consequence can be exerted upon or toward other physical forms. This confusion about the nature of the illusion can sometimes be employed as an excuse to avoid making an effort in life or from taking responsibility for consequences that arise from such effort ("nothing is actually real, so why make the effort"). At other times it can be a clever diversion when no other pleasing explanation for life's difficult outcomes can be found. While it may be broadly true to assert that "physical reality is an illusion" it is usually more accurate to state that "*my* perception and interpretation of physical reality is an illusion". Such a shift in emphasis provides a more honest attitude – especially in terms of being honest with ourselves – and places us in a position of curiosity and openness to learning rather than one of denial over the consequences of our own actions in the world. It also avoids that common view held about eastern perspectives that they are nihilistic and lacking in purpose. Reality, itself, is *not* an illusion. Rather, reality *is* whatever it *is* and it is our misplaced identity with aspects of reality which leads to misinterpretation, confusion and, ultimately, suffering. Understanding the constitution of illusion and how it causes that suffering is the path to unity and wholeness.

This brings us to the next form of illusion, which occurs in our emotional body (often referred to as the astral body) and is constructed of both emotions and the thoughtforms associated with emotions. This body is essentially a broad spectrum of subtler energies (finer than physical energies) which constitute the sum total of desires, attachments, reactions and activities of the emotional life. This vibrating body of energies remains, for the bulk of humanity, the major field of experience and interplay between the average human being and their environment. For most individuals in the world today, the familiar focus of interaction and response to the world around them is *through* their emotional energy body. While typically invisible to not only the naked eye but also to the instrumentation of material science, this body is definitely *sensed* and *registered* in the body and mind, and has a dynamic impact on experience. While awareness within the individual can be raised to higher states or more refined realms, conscious attention to this subtle body remains the major focus through which awareness relates to the world. Therefore, it presents an area of most difficulty for the lion's share of humanity. Human relationship, at this time in history, is largely *emotional* relationship and the majority of individuals can be more readily moved or influenced by an impassioned orator – even to the point of accepting a belief or position contrary to their own welfare.

    The majority of humanity is principally an 'emotional humanity'. As such, it is through this filter of desires, attachments, reactions and emotions which chiefly interferes with the capacity of consciousness to see reality accurately or to know its true Self. Every sensitivity, insecurity or tendency toward reaction in the individual's awareness acts as a distorting influence which constitutes the present field of primary illusion for consciousness. This illusion stemming from the emotional plane is described in esoteric terms as *glamour*. Where the indwelling consciousness believes that emotional qualities are a part of one's own identity so, too, will this identification constitute the field of glamour and illusion which results in suffering. Once again, wrong identification – this time to the emotions and desires – results in misdirected action. Until the indwelling consciousness can detach from the influences of the emotions it will not be able to free itself from the prison house of 'action and reaction'. As long as consciousness remains attached to the irresistible existence and influence of its emotional life – much like an actor unable to let go of their stage role – it suffers the trials and tribulations of that volatile and reactive body.

Various teachers through the ages have put forward a myriad of teachings on the need to detach from the emotional body and, particularly in this present world period, this step marks the next major accomplishment for humanity as a whole. This current era of astral/emotional entanglement has also been one of the most violent and self-destructive periods in human history. The unpredictable influence of the emotional plane, coupled with the immediacy of identification with that volatile and fluctuating nature, has immersed humanity in a labyrinthine maze of disparate and conflicting views, goals, purposes, opinions and motivations. It is even more important to realise that release from the confines and contortions of the emotional plane cannot be achieved through further activity or effort by the emotions themselves. As the Ageless Wisdom Teachings reveal, only a concerted effort to gradually raise the focus of consciousness onto the next higher plane – the mental body – will the effort be sufficient to free the individual from the tangles of the emotional nature. Such an effort does not involve any suppression or repression of the emotions. Rather, it is to gradually shift the habit of attention so that it operates through the higher mental body rather than through the life of the astral-emotional vehicle. This process of increasing detachment of identity from the emotions, along with an increasing understanding that the inner consciousness is merely the *experiencer* of emotions, eventually places the Soul in a position of mastery over those emotions.

Currently, for many, it is the emotional life which exercises control over the individual's life, driving them one way and then another according to the circumstances of the moment. The goal at this stage in history is to 'stand back' from identification with, and therefore the grip of, the emotions so as to be able to experience its contents and still remain free from its distorting interpretation of reality. The Soul, having achieved the realisation that it is not the emotions – albeit, intimately connected to the experience of them – can become freed from glamour and the imprisoning factors of the astral plane.

In *The Labours of Hercules*, the Tibetan Master D.K. provides a potent analysis of this challenge as it was portrayed through the familiar myth of the disciple Hercules slaying the many-headed hydra. For the purpose of illustration the lesson is worth briefly recounting here, although much detail is removed and is worth reading in full in the original text. As a whole, the story of the labours undertaken by Hercules describes the many tests and trials which await the disciple on their journey through the challenges of evolution and discipleship. Each labour represents a particular ordeal which the disciple must face, along with the key on how to unlock the trial. The eighth labour, slaying the Lernaean Hydra, represents that stage wherein the disciple is faced with the 'monster' which is their own emotional nature. It is interesting to note that the emotions are represented by the nine-headed hydra which wreaks havoc through the countryside and which finds its permanent abode in the dark fogs and mists of the stagnant and festering swamp of Lerna. This is an apt description of the emotional life, if we could but see it more clearly.

Hercules takes on this trial as any courageous warrior might – head on. Weapon at the ready and muscles taut the hero enters the dark swamp prepared for battle.

The confrontation ensues but every time Hercules destroys one head two more grow in its place. With each blow the creature grows stronger. Similarly, in direct confrontation with one's own emotions, any effort at suppression or repression feeds energy to that state and makes it even more pronounced in its hold over us. The indwelling consciousness, like Hercules, is faced with a challenge which only grows fiercer with the more effort that is applied directly toward subduing it. Nearly exhausted and overwhelmed by the monster, Hercules harkened back to the previous counsel of his Master: "We rise by kneeling; we conquer by surrendering; we gain by giving up". Casting his weapon aside, Hercules positioned himself before the raging beast and, lowering himself in humility onto one knee, grasped the writhing Hydra and lifted it up through the mists and fogs into the sunlight. Consumed by the power of the light, the Hydra withered and was destroyed. According to Alice Bailey, it was the sunlight, symbolising the light of "reason and compassion", which was needed to root out and overcome the qualities of the nine great vices in the emotional nature represented by the Hydra's heads. In this way the individual consciousness can be freed from the imprisoning effects of desires in the emotional vehicle. Through a new focus and polarisation into the higher mental body, the consciousness can utilise the fires of mind and the Soul to penetrate, disperse and root out attachments to the astral-emotional drives and desires. The Soul can then use this new and growing mental focus to understand that its nature is not the emotions, but that the emotional body is simply another tool for contacting the manifested world and to further reflect Its Divine Qualities into that sphere.

Such an achievement is difficult at this time since this body currently has the strongest influence on humanity. However, as more and more individuals move forward in this task it becomes easier for all to achieve. Such is the benefit and power of interconnectivity and interdependence. Likewise, progress along this stage is marked by a significant decrease in glamour for the indwelling consciousness itself – especially as the center of attention and identification becomes increasingly focused in the mental body rather than the astral-emotional body. The disciple is not yet out of the woods but the path has been cleared of some of the most obstinate hurdles, and the experience of life now stretches before them in a new and distinct way.

Having conquered *maya* on the material plane, and *glamour* on the astral-emotional plane, there now remains illusion as it constitutes an imprisoning factor on the mental plane. The third form of illusion is rightly termed *illusion* and forms an additional barrier that the indwelling consciousness must eventually overcome before it can achieve some degree of fuller control over its entire vehicle of manifestation, the personality, as well as to achieve a more sophisticated and refined expression of the Soul. This is by no means the stage of full liberation or enlightenment spoken of so often, but represents that stage where the indwelling consciousness can begin to experience *as a fact* the reality of its nature as whole and undivided. Until now, the Soul has been immersed in the glamours and illusions of its various bodies, and its identification and attachment to these vehicles of expression have made the distortions of those vehicles *its* distortions.

The mental plane is sometimes generally referred to as the 'plane of mind' and is home to both the 'lower' mind (within the personal identity) and the 'higher' mind (an aspect of the Divine Soul). It is home to those energetic structures which we typically refer to as ideas and ideals. More energetically subtle and refined than the astral-emotional body, this vehicle of expression is the repository of thoughtforms which are adopted and compiled from the multitude of beliefs, concepts and 'isms' that we encounter. An emotion or desire is an energetic expression emanating from the emotional body and this can influence or colour a further idea about that emotion on the mental plane. This thoughtform is added to the "idea" which we create about our own identity. To this we blend ideas and beliefs that we encounter in society or in our education and experience. With all of this we formulate an idea of ourselves on the mental plane which contains the blended assortment of any number of political, religious, economic or social viewpoints. Over time, this identity can completely change according to what new ideas are encountered and 'win out the day' to replace any other existing components within the identity. Today, "I" could be a Christian or a Buddhist but tomorrow "I" might become Muslim, Hindu or Jewish. "I" might prefer to be a capitalist this week but new knowledge may allow "me" to define myself as a socialist next week. One aspect of my identity might inform me that "I" am feminine but new sensations might encourage me to identify myself as masculine, or vice versa. This is all within the realm of personal identity to which the indwelling consciousness defines itself through this idea or that notion. These ideas of identity about itself provide the ring-pass-not of illusion within which we are each faced at any present moment in our lives. The more we 'identify' ourselves with the various physical, emotional and mental qualities of our vehicles the more we add to the idea of ourselves and, thus, to the layers of filters through which we perceive the world. The more detached we are with regard to this multifaceted central idea of ourselves the more we are capable of seeing reality-as-it-is. Conversely, the more fixed or unyielding we become in terms of our idea about who we are the more crystallised (fundamentalist, or even fanatical) may be our persona. This idea we hold about ourselves represents one of the major illusions on the mental plane facing the indwelling consciousness and it is the intensity of identification with this 'idea' which forms the prison walls within which consciousness remains incarcerated.

Through gradual detachment and decentralisation, the consciousness now stands free from its perceptions even though it continues to function fully through its vehicles in the physical, emotional and mental spheres. The challenge has been for consciousness to continue moving forward in the evolutionary process while persisting in the faith that its true nature is nondual and One with the Divine; not some 'blind faith' as espoused in so many religious corners today but a faith based on an inner Knowing resulting from experience, trial and application. Through strenuous effort and examination, consciousness begins to 'see' reality more directly and can advance to more clarity based on that progress.

Illusion on the mental plane remains an enigma to many and constitutes a field of understanding as yet unfamiliar to most. While it is not particularly difficult to describe the features of mental illusion, the illusion itself is often so deeply embedded

The Illusion of Separation

within personal identity that it can be exceedingly challenging to recognise its existence within oneself. It is the literal fabric of the notions we hold about ourselves which, in turn, provides the substance from which arise our motivations, characteristics, beliefs and endeavours. Complicating this task of discovery is the fact that the work of overcoming maya, glamour and illusion generally occurs simultaneously and an added challenge exists in making distinctions between the various types of illusion we have identified earlier, since the overcoming of each involves vastly different approaches.

It remains the responsibility and obligation of the sciences to investigate and incorporate those notions from the esoteric wisdoms into a better understanding of the psychological crisis of today. The possibilities exist wherein one day soon we might more fully understand not only the vehicle(s) and their functions in our experience but also the driving forces which have led humanity on to so much suffering.

The Illusion of Identity

> Our modern society is engaged in polishing and decorating the cage in which man is kept imprisoned.
>
> – *Swami Nirmalanada*

We arrive now at one of the most immediately consequential topics for the individual at this time – that the personal identity, and its *nom de plume* 'personality', constitutes for humanity a major obstacle to liberation. On the other hand, it also constitutes the vehicle through which that same liberation will be achieved. If it were as simple as removing or discarding the personality I am sure that we would have found many ways to have achieved that *en masse* by now. Instead, the task involves achieving 'mastery' over the fully developed personality and gradually perfecting its capacity to respond as a direct agent for the divine indwelling consciousness (the Soul).

In Esoteric Philosophy, 'personality' is described as being composed of the physical, astral (emotional) and mental bodies and, working together in a coordinated fashion, come together to express a unique overall quality which is the whole of the personality body itself. Each of the three lower bodies exhibits their own desire nature so that, at any point in time, a person may be responding to physical desire, an emotional or a mental desire. In most cases, any number of these various desires may be in agreement or in conflict with one another. The Soul, perfect on its own plane of existence, creates a new personality vehicle (a "personhood") in each incarnation on the physical plane and participates in the greater unfolding of human civilisation and evolution while, at the same time, works to bring its personality and the various bodies under the direction of Soul impulse. This complex process constitutes much of the Soul's millions of years-long evolution through reincarnation after reincarnation as it progressively builds vehicles with increasingly higher and more refined (and, therefore, responsive) qualities. Once some measure of 'influence' can again be applied to the personality from the Soul a more rapid progress can be made in the entire process toward liberation. It is not the Soul which is evolving in this process – since the Soul is already perfect on its own plane – but the Soul is learning to control and perfect its use of matter and, therefore, the bodies of manifestation on the lower planes (mental, astral and physical). It is along this epic journey that the *personality* of each individual experiences the circumstances of separation and long suffering that eventually leads to reuniting with the divine.

Part of the journey for a personality in any given life is the development of a 'personal identity'. Self-awareness of this 'construct' within oneself – achieved through self-analysis and self-reflection – can result in much faster progress along the Path. Such self-analysis requires that we have at least a basic understanding of *how* identity is constructed, from *what* it is constructed, and how it might function as an imprisoning factor to the indwelling consciousness.

It is also important to begin with a fundamental notion with regard to identity, or at least to hold temporarily as a premise to be tested, *that your personal identity is an illusion.* This is an idea which, for some, might elicit an initial scepticism or even derision. But it is worth bearing out the explanation to see if there might actually be a pot of gold at the end of this rainbow, or merely a trickster or rhetorical sleight-of-hand. A certain qualification can also be added to ensure that we do not start out on this journey together only to walk in separate directions. The type of illusion ascribed to the notion of 'personal identity' is not one of ultimate existence or to say that it is somewhat like a mirage that presents a desert sea before your eyes and yet disappears into the arid landscape when it comes time to plunge in. I make no reference to any ghost, or vapour, or trick of mirrors standing in place of where a 'personal identity' might dwell. This would be a misrepresentation of my words in the same way that the Buddhist notion of 'emptiness' has often been incorrectly interpreted as being a philosophy of nihilism or godlessness. I am eager to assert that an individual's 'personal identity' is very present and real, insofar as it has been 'put together' and constructed by that person and it is as towering and concrete as any prison wall could be. Nevertheless, what I am proposing when I forward the claim that 'personal identity' is an illusion is that it does not have an inherent life or existence *of its own*. That is to say, it exists and is sustained in its existence *only as long as* we each nourish it with the energies of our own convictions and beliefs. Where we hold it to be true in our minds that we are "this" individual with "these" particular ideals and qualities we sustain a very real and dynamic thoughtform in our minds *through* which we view and interpret the world. We are also very much limited and imprisoned by that same view of the world. If we hold to a notion that we are a Catholic, or a Hindu, or a communist, or a feminist (with all that any of these might entail) then any single event which unfolds will result in an entirely determined response according to dictates of that particular belief. In any singular event no one individual will be able to see reality-as-it-is. Instead, each person will generate their own reaction according to their own personal identities – formed as they are by individual beliefs and unique interpretations. As the Buddhist warrior monk Seosan Daesa once said, "If you wish to see the truth, then hold no opinions for or against anything". Most importantly, this necessarily includes not holding opinions about one's own personal identity since such a position could only colour our interpretation of reality around us. Not holding to a strong conviction about one's own personal identity begins to free the consciousness enough to experience reality-as-it-is. Why this should be so can be understood more clearly if we look more closely at what 'personal identity' is and how it forms.

We begin each life as an infant, a virtual *tabla rasa* of potentialities. In the best of circumstances, we are biologically 'intact' and imbued with consciousness and life. Yet we are more or less empty of social content and personal identity – lacking any significant degree of self-awareness, memories, social conditioning, gender influence, ideation, experience or ideals. We initially perceive the world around us but lack the classifications to categorise those perceptions, the concepts to identify or analyse them, or any language, speech or gesture to respond to their impact. Under normal conditions, an intense period of growth ensues in our early years where we begin to distinguish our surroundings and its occupants. We learn light from dark, wet from dry, safety from threat, pleasure from pain, and begin to build a rudimentary knowledge base in the brain about our environment. Note, however, that this early consciousness is already establishing a deeply engrained subjective perspective – that is, a locus of perception from which it views itself as separate from the world of objects and behaviours around it. A dualistic material perception and worldview is already conditioning the thought processes and displacing any possibility of an enduring nondualistic perspective. The primary imperative is to deal with the immediate and overwhelming flood of impulses from the developing material senses. As consciousness continues its journey, it takes its cues for survival from those around it and especially from those closest family members like parents, siblings and other extended family. The consciousness is rapidly building a picture of its 'place' in society and all the expectations and responsibilities that come with it. Ideas are introduced. Some relations become strained or even terminated while other relationships might flourish. New relations begin, then ensues primary school, more intimate encounters, some self-reflection, more responsibilities, and then memories of past successes and failures grow and are applied toward current behaviours and future expectations. We assemble more and more – adding an idea here, a responsibility there, until the best possible 'identity' can be constructed which will enable us to function and 'survive' in the world of material objects.

Everywhere along this timeline problems constantly arise. From the very beginning the indwelling consciousness is immersed in a nondual universe. Its very nature is undifferentiated from the 'other' (nondual) and its initial perspective emerges from an experience that is interconnected with all living things and all beings. However, submerged as it is in a rapidly growing vault of material dualistic perceptions, it is quickly overcome in the pressure to interpret its material surroundings and very soon loses the capacity to remain connected and focused to its own nature. To further exacerbate the challenge it has also had to create a mode of expression and response, as well as a vehicle for activity that is adapted to function and operate overwhelmingly through a dualistic (subject-object) interprettation of reality. The consciousness, through force of circumstances, has created and adapted to living within its own prison fortress of subject-object duality. It can sense its own nature of inclusiveness but cannot see or touch it. Instead, it only continues to experience, moment to moment, what appears as a factual and sensual separation between it and all other beings – including nature, and even God. This experience of separateness and disconnection is so pervasive and absolute that the consciousness has little recourse but to normalise this worldview and proceed from there.

This exploration so far gives a picture of the classical position within which consciousness is 'enveloped' and within which it must adapt and function. And yet, from the position of consciousness itself, there is no sense of this imprisonment at all – only the experience of trials and tribulations in life that it interprets to be coming *at* them from the 'outside' world. For consciousness, this is simply reality. In fact, knowledge of its nondual nature is so submerged by now that consciousness is, for almost the entirety of its long evolutionary journey, mostly oblivious to its true nature. It is only when nearing the latter stages of evolution, when the vehicle is becoming sufficiently sensitive to the impulses of the indwelling Soul, that a sense of the nondual reality starts to raise questions in the mind of the individual. One could be forgiven for thinking that perhaps this stage of newfound sensitivity represents the end of some epic journey; for the struggling consciousness has now started receiving a sense of the Truth about reality. But 'relief' is not the reward conferred at this stage of awakening. Rather, the consciousness is now buffeted relentlessly between its hard won habitual material worldview and the new but fleeting revelations of the divine, unified and nondual reality underlying its existence. Life for the indwelling consciousness, and for several of its lifetimes to come, becomes a burning ground for the crystallised identity, conditioned thoughts and entrenched views which have been defended for countless lives and which must be progressively dismantled and overcome. An increased suffering becomes a familiar companion even though this suffering represents a stage of real achievement in the overcoming of illusion. The life of an individual, immersed in the vast field of desires in the form world (physical, emotional and mental desires) is punctuated by moments of clarity, inspiration and revelation about the underlying unity. Paradoxically, rather than bringing solace, this contradiction in experience – alternating between an inner sense of unity and outer separation – necessarily leads to feelings of abandonment, isolation, alienation, manic-depressive episodes, deep depression, narcissism, self-pity, over-emphasis on the personal self and even suicidal thoughts. The day will come soon when psychologists and counsellors will need to distinguish between this type of 'existential' depression – arising from the growing interplay of the Higher and lower self – and depression that arises largely from biological or emotional imbalances arising from trauma or structural distortions in the personality itself. Modern psychology is more than equipped to deal with this latter condition while the former requires an entirely new approach since it is not an 'illness' *per se* as much as it is a "crisis of growth" which lies behind the individual's plight.

The path of suffering, while always present during the experience of separation, now intensifies where the indwelling consciousness begins to become aware of the inner schism. The major 'cure' going forward is a gradual decentralisation of the personal identity and a measured re-alignment of that identity with the whole rather than its part. This is accomplished significantly through meditation and service to others as the means to contact more regularly that internal divine nature as well as a full turning of the life and its activities toward service to others. Alice Bailey spoke highly of the 'Science of Service' as the preeminent science soon to dawn on our awakening civilisation:

> "You will all awaken some day to the realisation that the Science of Service is of greater importance than the Science of Meditation, because it is the effort and the strenuous activity of the serving disciple which evokes the soul powers, makes meditation an essential requirement, and is the mode – ahead of all others – which invokes the Spiritual Triad, brings about the intensification of the spiritual life, forces the building of the antahkarana, and leads in a graded series of renunciations to the Great Renun-

ciation, which sets the disciple free for all eternity".

With this awakening to the existence of the inner divine life the path of discipleship begins. The individual embarks on a life program of definitely 'decentralising' themselves through a deeper attention to the needs of others and the world. The disciple enters on the way of the crucifixion, progressively sacrificing everything to do with the 'little self' and the personal identity, and striving in every way to expand her contact and response to the 'higher self' – the indwelling consciousness on its own higher nondual plane.

Such a program of growth and expansion is not new and a prescription for this approach to life can be found throughout the various spiritual teachings of the ages. No less than 'the Golden Rule' itself provides the instruction *par excellence* for adopting a way of living that could bring an individual quickest to an *inner* experience and at-one-ment with their Source. "Do unto others, as you would have others do unto you" and "You shall love your neighbor as yourself" has been a central tenant of the Judeo-Christian ethic. Buddhist doctrine has taught that, "comparing oneself to others in such terms as 'Just as I am so are they, just as they are so am I,' he should neither kill nor cause others to kill". Hindus have found solace in the notion that "one should not behave toward others in a way which is disagreeable to oneself. This is the essence of morality. All other activities are due to selfish desire". Confucius bade his disciples "do not do to others what you do not want them to do to you". Mohammad instructed his adherents that "not one of you is a believer until he loves for his brother what he loves for himself". Jainism accepts that "a man should wander about treating all creatures as he himself would be treated". Spanning a period of more than 5000 years and across a multitude of civilisations this notion of re-orienting oneself from an identity grounded in self-love and self-importance toward a decentralised expression of loving and serving others remains, to this day, the *central* teaching of the ages. If these common teachings are to be looked at closely and carefully it can be seen that the *psychological* effect of putting such an injunction into practice would serve to re-orient the worldview of the personal identity and generate a unitive disposition emphasising one's nature and existence as part of the Whole. In one sense this appears quite revolutionary in terms of how diverse and dissimilar religious groups have similarly gravitated to this common formula for spiritual living. They universally speak to the individual cultivation of a mindset of which the result is unity, cooperation and peace.

Regardless of the age, culture, societal period, language, or customs throughout history this notion of 'seeing others as yourself' rises time and again as a life preserver for a humanity set adrift on the waves of time, space and form – a humanity bound like a suffering Prometheus by the chains of dualism and materiality. Our myths and legends repeat this theme endlessly, providing salvation to any who might choose to hear and take the first steps toward unity. "Love one another as yourself". Taken unquestioningly as a command from on High we perhaps miss the obvious point that this simple morsel of Truth describes reality as *those* teachers saw it, and that such an activity was the means by which we could experience that divine reality for ourselves. Arising from their own perceptions of the world as unified and nondual, they provide humanity with a quick and sure path for salvation. This consistent doctrine through the ages speaks to the fact that each of these great sages witnessed the nature of reality as One, and that the Path or Way forward for humanity out of its present state of separation and disconnection was to re-instate that relationship of interdependence and interconnectedness in every aspect of our daily lives. To begin to "treat one another as yourself" is to begin to represent yourself as part of the One. It could be no other way, and any teaching that would emphasise the opposite – promoting separation and division – operates against the very foundation of human nature.

The Illusion of Identity

Another way to view this idea is to consider the worldview from which the teachings were presented. For the Christ, "I and My Father are one". Krishna proclaimed to his disciple Arjuna that, "He who experiences the unity of life sees his own Self in all beings, and all beings in his own Self, and looks on everything with an impartial eye; he who sees Me in everything and everything in Me, him shall I never forsake, nor shall he lose Me". Confucius declared that, "The oneness of Infinity is the source of the peace and harmony within me. How can anyone take it away from me"? For Shankaracharya, "Whatever is perceived in the universe is the immutable Lord alone; there exists nothing that is other than He. I am He; thou art He; all that exists is He. Give up the delusion of separateness". From virtually every major spiritual tradition, we encounter primary spiritual teachings which speak to a perspective espousing the Oneness of all existence. For what reason, then, should we attempt to interpret the remainder of their teachings in any context other than that which asserts that the nature of humanity is one? Where the various teachings or instructions have not openly or directly described the fundamental Oneness of humanity, an honest and sincere reading should at least grant that we should interpret the parables, axioms and methods of those teachers within a *context* that accepts the fundamental truth of Oneness. It is difficult to imagine that any principle or philosophy emanating from this collective of spiritual teachers could offer any path forward that did not end in a nondual understanding of the world and ourselves. The challenge faced by each and every one of them was to communicate an understanding of reality which did not sound either contradictory or paradoxical to the common citizen – a challenge which still exists today. It is a profound moment in history, perhaps, that we can now begin to look back at those same teachings from all the major traditions and see them align significantly with a nondual science and reality that we are only now beginning to comprehend. To "love one another as yourself" was not some sentimental aphorism but was the very prescription for psychological and spiritual evolution in the human being. It is an activity, when put into expression, which brings about a deeper awareness of our own nature as spiritual beings. It is salvation itself. The universe is one united whole, and the only true way to participate in the manifestation of that must be through *unity*.

It is important to return to our examination of personal identity. Having examined a few factors in relation to the personality, a picture has begun to form of what exactly constitutes the personal identity and how it functions as a virtual prison for the indwelling consciousness. Essentially, identity is created in the mind as a complex thoughtform and held relatively stable through repetition, conviction of beliefs, societal structures, familial influences, social norms and rules, and the refinement of expressive characteristics designed to provide a sense of individuality, belonging and 'existence' in the physical world that we perceive.

At times, family tradition will dominate an individual's identity construct causing the adoption of their political, religious and/or social values as one's own. In other instances, the individual identity may form as a rebellion against those same traditions. Where fear, suppression or violence influences early development the identity formation will either build protective or evasive mechanisms into its persona (even though those mechanisms may be detrimental in the long run) or, alternatively, adopt those negative traits as a template for dealing with others – regardless of whatever features, beliefs or qualities are built into the matrix of being a 'separate self'. It is further underwritten and substantiated by the dualistic sensory experience of physical material existence. Thus, the identity becomes deeply conditioned toward sustaining and refining its material existence and often never even imagines to question the essential reality of that existence – even though, as we have just described, its identity (thoughtform) is nothing more than a temporary conglomeration of ideas, habits, beliefs and perspectives.

This deeply conditioned 'idea' of oneself exists merely as a set of brain waves, coordinated into a coherent set of impressions or notions about oneself and hardly even registers as a measurable electrical charge on the physical plane. Yet, its all-encompassing embrace creates a virtual prison for the indwelling consciousness. This consciousness, through the process of ongoing and deep conditioning, believes so thoroughly in its own construct that it can't even imagine itself to be anything *but* that identity. The road to liberation from this labyrinthine enclosure is long and complex – yet achievable. History has recorded many great disciples who have wrestled against this conditioning, transcended the personal separate identity, and who have charted a course for others to follow. This illusion which is the 'separate self', the 'I', exists for each of us only insofar as the consciousness remains convinced that it is so and thus sustains its form. And it is the existence of a separate illusory identity which results in the experience of disconnection from the world, from each other and from God.

Esoteric philosophy has expressed repeatedly that only one fundamental 'sin' exists for humanity – the 'sin of separation'. This original primordial event – the separation of humanity from awareness of its own divine nature – marks a period in the distant past of humanity's evolution where consciousness first became self-aware and, as a result, separate and distinct from its Source. This activity of mind to examine itself in order to know itself 'set the pilgrim on its way', only to return to its Source once the long path of evolution could make possible the achievement of full self-realisation and liberation as a divine being. According to the Ageless Wisdom Teachings, consciousness begins from an unrealised state of unity with the divine Source. It goes forth under the Plan of God into an individuated state, *identified* with the separate material form that it creates as a vehicle of manifestation. While identified with its material form, consciousness experiences the suffering and pain of separation which acts as the stimulus to seek and to grow – to know who or what it is and why it is here. Life after life, incarnation after incarnation, the Soul (consciousness) advances incrementally in its awareness of the nature of life. Nearing the end of that long evolutionary journey consciousness comes to understand itself as the indwelling divine nature and gradually frees itself from the grip of material form life. This revelation eventually leads to liberation from that material form and, ultimately, a return to unity with the divine Source. It retains its individuated state as a fully self-realised divine Being, participating now consciously as an individual expression within in the Plan of God.

The Illusion of Identity

It is an interesting and revealing exercise to recognise the existence of a personal identity as the cause of separation and that this separation is the basis of our suffering. In fact, a careful and sincere examination will reveal that all negative emotions can be found to have roots in the belief that we are separate from one another. Fear, envy, greed, jealousy, anger, loneliness, remorse, selfishness and arrogance are only the beginning of a long list of characteristics which arise from the belief that we are separate from the world and from each other. If these perceptions of separateness were to cease entirely then so, too, would those negative characteristics cease to arise. In Buddhism, this idea is found in the notion of *dependent co-arising* (pratityasamutpada) and illustrates that our suffering arises out of our illusory views of the world. This idea also finds its demonstration in the lives of those advancing members of humanity who, nearing the gates of liberation, become largely freed of selfish actions and relate to their fellow beings mainly through the lens of compassion, inclusiveness, love and truth. As their awareness broadens to include more of the Whole they are increasingly influenced by the experience of the underlying unified reality. Their only course of expression, if they are to express the truth that they see, is to manifest that inclusiveness in every word and deed. Conversely war and strife will never end for humanity (and may even threaten to end humanity itself) until we can come to understand that we are fundamentally part of one divine existence – one world, united and inseparable. The only way forward for humanity, if it is to survive and flourish, is through unity and love. There is no other way.

This brings us back to the issue of mental illusion. Illusion on the mental plane is fundamentally challenging since it is the plane upon which maya and the glamours of the lower planes converge with further ideas about ourselves us to form a coherent persona. This persona includes within it various contradictions and inner conflicts which further give rise to neuroses and dysfunction in the personality. This is where the fields of psychology and psychiatry have played an important role in helping the indwelling consciousness to reform or rehabilitate the 'ideas' which it has adopted in the creation of its identity. Psychology has made great strides over the last century in understanding the appearance of these behaviours and how they might treat or modify the expression of those behaviours. What remains to be more fully discovered is both how this entire matrix of the personal identity is a self-constructed illusion as well as how that illusion can eventually be placed in the right context in relation to the observing consciousness. One wonders, for example, how much of depression be ameliorated through an understanding that the crisis of depression may actually be a hallmark of growth and expansion beyond the boundaries of the existing identity rather than a dysfunction or psychological pathology requiring pharmaceutical intervention. That does not make the experience of depression any easier to bear but it can dramatically alter our understanding of the true crisis behind this "moment preceding a new revelation". This can also significantly alter how we determine treatment in such instances. Are we mis-construing a spiritual crisis or crisis of meaning and purpose for a biological or chemical imbalance? While they may be coincidental, we still do not understand which feature of the crisis is causative. Is the production of stress hormones causing depression and withdrawal from one's current life circumstances or is the stress of the unfulfilling limits of one's own identity causing the production of a depressive chemistry in the brain? While many individuals can find some degree of benefit by the introduction of pharmaceutical intervention, we might also witness many people achieve a deeper and longer lasting benefit by making fundamental changes in the way they understand their lives and define themselves. What is probably certain is that without this fundamental transformation in thinking about oneself it is likely impossible to get away from the depressive state entirely. This self-created prison will always linger in the background of the psyche since the psyche has not made a significant enough break from its previously confining thoughtforms.

We currently live in one of the greatest periods of psychological depression ever recorded. It is time for us to grasp the nature of this suffering and to understand that a significant amount of it may be rooted in the minds of those whose consciousness has become overly inhibited by the constraints of their own identity construction. The identity is simply too inadequate to express the growing consciousness within. The consciousness of humanity is expanding tremendously at this time in history and our individual concept of who we are is not keeping apace. Therefore, the prison walls are feeling tighter for an increasing number of people and this is leading to mass psychological suffering and depression. Medication will not be the answer, although it can serve to temporarily 'soften' the intensity of the crisis which consciousness experiences, thereby reducing the sense of imprisonment and depression. Our new approach needs, instead, to expand our sense of identity and idea of who we are. It will not suffice forever to continue to merely temper our pain with drugs, sex, gambling, work and more. We must reach out to re-define who we are and what we can be. We must find that experience of oneness and divinity that can help us to understand how to live a new way.

Herein lies the double-edged sword. The Soul (consciousness) comes into material incarnation and builds for itself vehicles of expression on each of the various material planes. Through continued experience it expands its capacity for expression while, at the same time, coordinates the various bodies into one coherent and dynamic persona – all the while deepening its identification with that persona. As its identity grows so, too, does its identification with that persona grow. The Soul, to its benefit, has created a wonderful manifestation through which it can function reasonably on all the lower planes of existence (mental, emotional and physical). However, this intimate identification with its vehicles also makes it subject to every crisis and blow which befalls its prized vehicles. The Soul is both master architect and inhabitant of the architecture at once. The actor has forgotten that it is only a role and not only plays the part but now lives the part with full conviction. At the same time it is compelled to suffer the joys and sorrows, the successes and failures, which befall its character on stage.

Notwithstanding the real and significant presence of physiological and neurological imbalance which can be the source of some depression it is undeniable that the sufferer of depression is, in many cases, inundated by a type of overwhelming self-focus, self-loathing and self-disregard. This narcissistic orientation feels sufficiently justified to the unfortunate victim and yet often appears wholly unjustified or over-emphasised by those friends and counsellors who seek to render help and support. Whatever the challenges are that confront every individual in the normal course of life – the loss of a job or relationship, rejection by a friend, or the instance of an opportunity missed – such events can plunge the seemingly hapless depressant into a spiral of self-condemnation, self-criticism and, eventually, an inescapable self-reinforcing swamp of self-pity. Each strengthening reference to the misfortunes of the little personal self inflates and fortifies the lack of self worth. It is this burgeoning Hydra of 'me' and 'mine' which confronts the indwelling consciousness. The self-focused persona begins to detach from reason by creating a self-reinforcing feedback loop. The suffering individual detests both themselves and their life situation and, yet, feels immobilised to make it any better. All life around them is witnessed as better than what they deserve or can attain. Where this incessant rumination on oneself and its moment to moment needs becomes too overwhelming tragedy ensues and no amount of medical or pharmaceutical intervention can really suffice to 'cure' the person. However, where the inner Hercules can be helped to see that the challenge facing him is not the intensity of daily emotions or beliefs that binds him but the fact that it is his attachment to his current identity which keeps him enthralled. It is the totality of the "I must be this" and "I must accomplish that" and "I must look like this" which, when formed into a coherent identity, is a life-destroying Hydra which cannot be overcome by merely attacking this or that head. The endeavour of creating a personal identity must be seen and then lifted up as a whole into the sun for examination. It is not this feature or that feature which, when resolved will eventually end depression, but one has to see that it is the whole reflex of creating and inhabiting an 'identity' which is behind the isolating and alienating experience. In that instance of revelation depression and the cause of depression can potentially be shattered. It is through the de-centralising influence of the higher divine nature which can, quite effectively, obliterate the depressive tendencies of the self-focused 'little self'. Depression does not, and cannot, exist where the personality and its identity is reoriented toward the expression of the Soul's purpose through service. This has always been true for those who understood this ancient law and it can be through a deeper understanding of the existence of the inner divine Soul in every individual which could lead the fields of psychology and psychiatry to develop new and more lasting approaches to mental health and depression. This does not discount the use of pharmaceuticals used to manage some of the characteristics of mental health challenges. However, no full amelioration of depression can occur where the original cause of suffering turns out to be the result of attachment to identity.

Psychology has advanced considerably in the west and yet, relative to the progress made in some eastern traditions, it remains a relatively young science. It has been tasked with the exploration and understanding of mind and, therefore, the person. It is further challenged to bring therapeutic support to those whose faculties of mind have suffered breakdown or illness. What handicaps the study of mind and personality in the west is that there does not yet exist a coherent and definitive theory for consciousness. What is this "awareness" which creates an identity as well as a vehicle of expression for itself? This is an important point worth noting. If pressed the therapist will be first to admit that no clear understanding of consciousness exists. Consciousness, functioning through its vehicle(s) of expression (physical, emotional and mental), is like the driver of a car navigating through a complex system of traffic. Without understanding the purpose or ultimate goal of the driver, the science of mind has only had to rely on observations of the dodging and darting about of their various vehicles in order to understand anything about the indwelling driver. To be certain, an enormous body of knowledge has been collected and analysed with regard to mind and its operations. And yet, little remains understood about the fundamental nature, origin and purpose of consciousness itself. On the other hand, Esoteric Philosophy has begun to provide a coherent presentation of both the nature of consciousness and its evolution and purpose. The fact that not every conclusion of esotericism can be measured by empirical tools should not be cause for concern since consciousness may not be of a dimension measurable by present day science. Nevertheless, the ideas presented are robust and coherent within the world of *meaning* (an area within which science admittedly has little capacity, or license, to draw conclusions) and can be accessed only through the instruments of intuition and reason. These tools are now rapidly aiding honest investigators and thinkers around the world in dispelling those illusions which have kept humanity imprisoned and restrained. The time for emancipation is fast approaching.

One of these tools for emancipation is meditation and it has become one of the fastest growing methods of self-inquiry in the western world. In the east, meditation has been a central tool for the study of consciousness and the 'self' stretching back thousands of years. To know the Self is to know the world and meditation is essential to that effort. There are countless forms of meditation with new techniques continuing to be invented daily. But few techniques are designed to really bring the individual rapid growth and self-awareness. Some examples of popular practices in the west include Buddhist Vipassana meditation or the Maharishi Mahesh Yogi's mantra-centred technique called Transcendental Meditation (popularised by the Beatles and the Beach Boys throughout the 1960s and early 1970s). My own experience with meditation began over 30 years ago and included some experimentation with the techniques listed above. Although it was the discovery of a technique called Transmission Meditation in the 1980s (presented to the world in the 1970s by British esotericist and author Benjamin Creme) which led to a consistent practice for me that continues to this day. Transmission Meditation has been, for me, a dynamic vehicle for both service in the outer world and expansion of my own inner awareness in the inner world. Each individual must find their own approach and, if possible, seek to expand their capacities for inner knowing and inner connectedness. An effective method of meditation is an absolute necessity in the search for the limitation of one's own identity and in overcoming the illusions of that identity.

Dis-unity and Suffering

> It is not impermanence that makes us suffer. What makes us suffer is wanting things to be permanent when they are not.
>
> – Thich Nhat Hanh

The 20th century was a period wracked by violence, and the first decades of the 21st century have evidenced more barbarity and suffering than probably any other time in recorded history. The sheer scale of global destruction, blind genocide and sheer human catastrophe is approaching levels beyond description. It is true that most rational and balanced individuals find suffering unpleasant, although the cause of suffering for each may be vastly different. While many seem able or even willing to bear the weight of suffering few would actually invite it as a way of life or welcome it as a desired experience. Physical pain is known to anyone with a nervous system while there are few who have not also experienced suffering in some mental or emotional way. All of this begs a most important question: how can we be so universally opposed and averse to suffering yet fail so miserably at preventing it in the world or understanding the reason why we perpetuate the conditions of suffering?

Dis-unity and Suffering

In *Esoteric Astrology*, Alice Bailey wrote of each planet in our solar system as constituting unique schools for the evolution of Souls and civilisations. In the case of Earth – *The School of Magnetic Response* – there is a particular challenge for its evolving Souls to master the task of 'adjudicator' between the polar opposites. In this work of synthesising the world of dualities, successful candidates are granted the title of "The graduates of painful endeavour". I could think of no more apt title describing the long suffering journey of humanity from bondage (in dualistic thinking) to liberation (into nondual awareness). Bailey also wrote that pain is a "purifying agent, employed by the Lords of Destiny, to bring about liberation" (*Externalisation of the Hierarchy*). It is during those periods of pain and suffering wherein we experience the most maturation and growth, and where the veils of illusion are most readily penetrated and shattered. It is the very process of the evolution of consciousness, immersed in the illusions of the dualistic material world, that pain and suffering act as the engines of growth toward eventual liberation and return to the blissful experience of the One.

In the first of his Four Noble Truths the Buddha described one of the most succinct and complete statements about the experience of consciousness in the physical world. His words are often abbreviated to the simple phrase, "Life is suffering". However, it might serve some purpose to examine the original phrase in its totality as it is presented in the *Dhammacakkappavattana Sutta*: "Now this, bhikkhus [monks], is the noble truth of suffering: birth is suffering, aging is suffering, illness is suffering, death is suffering; union with what is displeasing is suffering; separation from what is pleasing is suffering; not to get what one wants is suffering; in brief, the five aggregates subject to clinging are suffering". This statement is packed with clues regarding the causes of suffering. Of particular interest is the last phrase which asserts that "the five aggregates subject to clinging are suffering".

In modern language we would interpret this clinging as *attachment* to the 'things' we experience. Our attachment to things can even include our own identity if it is something that comes into the realm of our experience. And what is it within us that is "subject to clinging?" The Buddha would assert that it is the "five aggregates" (or *Skandhas*, as they are known in eastern traditions) which are the features within us that provide the propensity for attachment. These *Skandhas* were dealt with at great length in the *Pali Canon*, and the Buddha described these five aggregates as *form* (matter), *sensation* (sensory experience), perception (recognition, naming), *mental formations* (ideas about things) and *cognisance* (discrimination/discernment). These aspects of our awareness make us vulnerable to attachment since they all create the illusion of separation and subject-object relationship to the world. Each of these, in their own way, constitutes a means of identifying something as an object or 'thing'. We are "thing-making" creatures. Even our thoughts are 'things' which we cling to as building bricks for the construction of our identity. As a result, we are confined within a thick wall of attachments to the products of our thinking and making. By identifying separate objects through the five aggregates we become increasingly dis-united – our personas being merely an assemblage of these fragments.

Inundated with a wide range of physical, emotional and mental characteristics the indwelling consciousness creates successive identities from the broad spectrum of possibilities in its search to know itself. However, having limited equipment through which to experience, the journey to self-awareness and liberation becomes one of repeated appropriation of one feature of identity after another followed by the subsequent pain arising from the separation inherent in that identity-making process. The very act of assuming an identity, if even for the best intentions, is itself an act of separating oneself from the Whole. The more we seek to know 'ourselves' the more we create some separate version of identity. The more we create identity, and the more we attach to those beliefs and ideas which constitute the identity, the more separation is created leading to further suffering. This pain acts as a purifying and liberating force leading to the break down, in some measure, of the structure of identity. During each period of 'break down' we remove or 'let go' of some features (whether they be ideas of relationship, religion, politics or any number of characteristics built into the identity) and we continue on in life, often adding new beliefs in the place of the old discarded ones. As long as we continue to attach ourselves to the complex of new thoughts, beliefs and ideas so will we formulate the circumstances upon which the next inevitable round of pain and suffering will unfold.

This does not, however, need to be the final fate of humanity. The Buddha, along with mystics and teachers throughout the ages, has taught of a way forward beyond this cycle of separation and pain. This Path, in whatever form it has been presented throughout the ages, involves the cessation of the identity-making process and the cultivation of detachment from the vehicles which have been mistakenly appropriated as aspects of personal identity. Such notions may sound virtually impossible to attain – and even heretical to some – and, yet, many adventurous Souls have put into practice these techniques and cultivated the achievement of detachment. Many have experienced revelatory insights into their own nature. In some instances, the vista of nondual reality has revealed itself to the pilgrim able to detach from their identity. This is not the detachment of suppression, abandonment or repression but involves the gradual realisation of the unreality and irrationality of the separateness that 'appears' to exist. Such detachment allows the individual consciousness to look out at its various vehicles as mere instruments of contact to the physical, emotional and mental planes of existence. Detachment provides the necessary perspective allowing the indwelling consciousness freedom to know itself as the Observer rather than the thing observed.

Identify with the body and consciousness will suffer when it experiences the body injured or harmed. Identify with the emotions and consciousness will suffer when a negative emotion confronts it. Identify with a belief or idea and consciousness will suffer if the belief is attacked or discredited. Much the worse it is, indeed, where the suffering consciousness returns the suffering in kind to those whom it feels dealt the original blow. If we could see the history of humanity in these terms we would see not only individuals but entire societies waging great wars against one another, all for the sake of their particular notions and temporary identifications of the period. A crusader against the moor, whites against blacks, capitalists versus socialists...the history of mankind is a history of the battle between opposing ideas and polar opposites. These various 'sides' pass soon enough into the history books and

Dis-unity and Suffering

the evolution of ideas, through time, provides a fresh ground upon which to both identify and subsequently disagree again with one another – sparking yet another era of strife, war and suffering.

Little can be done to overcome this suffering until consciousness can begin to detach from its identification with the lower natures and move upward; first to the light of mind and then further to the higher Light of the Divine Soul itself. By lifting the polarisation of consciousness from the astral/emotional upward to the mental plane, and then from a mental focus to Soul focus, will the individual be able to step beyond the struggles of duality and begin to see itself as part of the nondual Whole. In *Discipleship in the New Age, Volume I,* Bailey describes the challenges which face the individual who strives to overcome emotions and advance toward mental polarisation.

> The disciple faces the world but he faces it from the level of the soul, looking clear-eyed upon the world of human affairs. "In the world, yet not of the world" is the right attitude—expressed for us by the Christ. Increasingly must the normal and powerful life of the emotional, astral, desire and glamorous nature be controlled and rendered quiescent by the life of the soul, functioning through the mind. The emotions which are normally self-centred and personal must be trans-

muted into the realisations of universality and impersonality; the astral body must become the organ through which the love of the soul can pour; desire must give place to aspiration and that, in its turn, must be merged in the group life and the group good; glamour must give place to reality, and the pure light of the mind must pour into all the dark places of the lower nature. These are the results of mental polarisation and are brought about by definite meditation and the cultivation of the meditative attitude.

What is apparent in this view is that regardless of the actual 'right' or 'wrong' of any particular idea it is the *identification* of the indwelling consciousness with the emotions and the ideas of the lower mind which give rise to suffering. Detachment is the antidote to wrong identification – a type of inoculation against the imprisoning effects of identity-building.

In whatever manner one might wish to view this question, it remains difficult to deny that every attempt by consciousness to define itself in terms of some 'form' (whether physical, emotional or mental) constitutes a separative act, regardless of how subtle or gross is the attempt. It is not the correctness or incorrectness of any idea that is central here but it is the adoption of, and identification with, those ideas as defining one's 'self' which constitutes the generative force behind suffering. For this reason our wonderful home, this planet, remains the school of 'painful endeavour'. It is not because we face such a variety of ideas and notions. Indeed, it is the manifestation of such diversity which is our gift to the Cosmos. But it is our immersion into matter and our subsequent identification with those objects of our minds which makes this journey one of such profound suffering. It is this journey which teachers through the ages have attempted to reveal so that we might more rapidly find our way home to that state of awareness which no longer knows any division.

Unity and Language

> Everyone Is God speaking.
> Why not be polite and Listen to Him?
>
> – *Hafiz*

A few words are necessary here with regard to language. In particular, how language and the use of language relates to nonduality and Oneness as well as the separative effect that language can have on how our consciousness interprets the world. The Ageless Wisdom Teachings define speech as 'concretised thought'. As such, the control of speech is really facilitated through the control of one's own thoughts and ideas. Wherever the thoughts are permitted to stray – whether generated by the fickle play of emotions or the result of focused determination – so, too, will be the lines upon which speech will tend to manifest. If thoughts are haphazard and extreme so, too, will the quality of speech follow. Alternatively, where thoughts are carefully constructed and intelligently employed, likewise will speech follow suit.

The thoughts behind speech, in turn, are stimulated by the stream of information coming into the brain and mind through the senses. These impressions provide the basic 'matrix' upon which more subtle and refined notions are built. Ideas, beliefs and concepts enter our field of perception and these influences modify both our understanding of the world as well as our place in it.

Our first instances of awareness in the world generate a need – small at first, but increasingly imperative – to communicate and relate to others. This imperative is initially satisfied through hand gestures and vocal grunts but that soon becomes insufficient to express the fullness of the rapidly expanding awareness. Eventually, we reach out for language and adopt that form most readily available to us from our familiars and society. As we grasp language we expand our capacity considerably to express the thoughts and impressions forming in our mind. At the same time, language influences immensely the thoughts and ideas that we have about the world and, most critically, about our own identity. Therefore, it is important to understand not only what language brings us in terms of ideas about the world but to appreciate how language defines us – for it is the language we employ to define our identity which later becomes part of the prison from which we must eventually break free.

Language is one of the most direct adaptable instruments for describing relationship. Whether that relationship is between two individuals or represents entire civilisations and generations, language is the

Unity and Language

very thread that knits together the fabric of relating. It can come in many shapes and sizes and exhibit a broad range of characteristics. Language can be spoken, written, carved in stone and even broadcast using hand gestures, smoke signals, radio waves or bursts of laser light. Any number of symbols can be employed to represent individual sounds which when pieced together produce words, pictograms, hieroglyphs and more to represent complex ideas or concepts.

For the purposes of this discussion, language can be seen as that essential tool which is enlisted to bridge the gap between two or more subjects. Moreover, language not only bridges the gap between subjects it can, by definition, *sustain* that gap. That is, while it is used to relate to one another, its use reinforces the perception that such a gap exists. In this sense it is a dividing force. This is a fundamental consideration since the absolute ending of separation would also include the end of any need for language and communication as we understand it in present day terms. The use of language will one day need to be superseded by a type of "global awareness". Where psychologist Carl Jung spoke of a 'collective unconscious', humanity will need to enter into a 'collective consciousness' which will need to be unfolded from the higher capacities and perceptions latent within us. One can even infer that a state of ultimate conscious unity is also a state of absolute awareness of reality-as-it-is.

So the beginning of separation was also the beginning of language (or the need for language). The form and complexity that communication takes depends entirely upon the degree to which consciousness can manifest its nature through the vehicles it creates. Where the vehicle is basic or insufficient so, too, will be the methods of communication. For a mineral stone or single-celled amoeba simple chemical or electrical signals can communicate atttracttion, repulsion or other basic relationships with other forms of life. In the plant kingdom, communication involves colour or scent. In the animal kingdom, communication can include colour and scent but also incorporate sound or patterns of movement. In the human kingdom, complex expressions of consciousness will require sophisticated languages and intricate methods of communication (i.e., sacred geometry, esoteric art, mathematics, etc). Human beings are also capable of responding to the less complicated signals of the lower kingdoms but require a significantly more complex discourse in order to articulate and convey ideas known only to the higher reaches of abstract mind and beyond. As consciousness develops ever more adequate forms for expressing its nature the capacity to understand its own nature also improves. Thus, consciousness forces the evolution of the form side of life and, in turn, the expanding form evolves to accommodate a greater expression for consciousness. This feedback loop exists throughout all the kingdoms in nature but in the human kingdom – the kingdom of 'mind' – this process has been facilitated immensely through language.

Language, at this stage in human history, has been one of the important stimulants behind the evolution of consciousness. As the capacity for higher abstract thought has matured across a greater portion of our species so, too, does the need arise for an ever more refined vocabulary. As vocabulary and the use of more complex symbols expand (and we are now approaching that moment in history where such an expansion is again necessary) we will need to remain aware of the negative effects that language has on the formation of identity. We already see some aspects of this in the use of mobile phones and its power to increase communication around the world and between one another. While it is true to say that it has increased our capacity to pass information to one another it has not necessarily increased our expression of empathy, compassion and unity. In fact, some would argue that mobile phone use has decreased these qualities and, at least initially, increased our capacity to express disdain or dis-unity with one another. Connectivity is not a substitute for unity although, with the right understanding, it could become an instrument for cultivating unity.

It is difficult to imagine one word in the English language which could have such a powerful effect on the human mind so as to imprison it in one simple concept or idea. Worse yet is the fact that this single word has also been one of the major drivers behind the evolution and expansion of consciousness and its capacity to express itself. This lone word has been at the forefront of bringing forth incredible developments from consciousness and yet serves as that constraining force which constitutes the barrier beyond which the indwelling consciousness regularly confronts and must eventually transcend. I am speaking no less than of the word "I".

Few other words could be said to contain so much power as is found in the word "I". This simple pronoun captures within its influence all genders, races, religions, nationalities and political affiliations which have existed or will exist in our civilisation. Imagine any other word or letter containing all of this. When used in a sentence it is always capitalised whereas other pronouns like 'he' or 'she' are rarely afforded this distinction. When any individual employs the use of this word they are indicating to the listener that a single solitary being is here in existence – 'I am' or 'I exist'. As simple as this term appears on the surface it is used by both the subject (the speaker) and the object (the listener) to each define themselves. "I" declares to anyone listening that a center of consciousness is present *in a form*. This is the key to understanding the power of "I" since it represents the declaration that consciousness has taken on some form which is observable and definable within the material world.

The further power in "I" is that it is, for the human being, a declaration of the observable materialisation of Divine Consciousness in *form*. It is, in every instance of use, a unique expression of some fragment of the Divine which stands behind the manifested universe – a distinct wave upon the ocean. That sum total of thoughts, emotions and physical parts which are knit together to fabricate the complete form of any particular "I" provides the central vehicle of expression for each incarnating Soul today. The totality of "I" for each instance of consciousness serves as the evolving chariot on the path to manifesting and expressing that individuality, to whatever degree this 'identity' can be adapted or expanded to the needs of that indwelling consciousness. Nevertheless, each declaration of "I" is also an individual and unique appearance of the same common underlying divinity.

Therein lays the path of separation and suffering for consciousness. Because of its incapacity to fully comprehend its own divine nature, consciousness is reduced to defining its 'I-ness' according to the limitations and limits of its various vehicles (mental, emotional and physical). The "I", by definition, is a statement of separateness from others and the world and leaves the consciousness ensnared in the idea of itself as somehow 'apart' from creation. Built into this isolating and individualising process is also the suffering which impels the consciousness forward in growth until this illusion of separation can be broken. Isolation, loneliness and alienation are only by-products of the true cause of suffering, which turns out to be a belief in the existence of a separate "I". This is why the sense of loneliness and isolation can persist even when an individual is in a room full of close friends and relatives. As long as the idea of "I" exists then the experience of separateness must also be present.

The final stage of evolution for consciousness in the human kingdom approaches when the illusion of this separate 'self' – this separate "I" – is surmounted. For consciousness, a growing experience of interconnectedness arises and a fuller expression of divine qualities unfolds. The Soul must gain mastery over its lower separative bodies and their desires, and bring the lower vehicles into a coherent alignment. The qualities of consciousness – unity and wholeness – are expressed through traits such as service, selflessness, empathy and compassion. The advanced man or woman now fully manifests an individual expression of the Divine and

Unity and Language

retains a constant cognisance of their oneness with both humanity and all of creation. The final stage of evolution in the human kingdom sees the relinquishment and total renunciation of the pronoun "I" ("not my will, but Thy Will be done") and the Divine Individual now surrenders all final beliefs in separation. They have become a unique manifestation of the Divine, now serving humanity as a whole and working toward the salvation of all those remaining within the prison house of "I".

Such is both the necessity of "I", as a structure for the progression of evolution, and the eventual demise of "I" and its renunciation. The ongoing challenge for humanity is that we are a combination of a formless consciousness identified with vehicles of form. This somewhat schizophrenic state generates a kind of existential tension in life which combines a desire to explore the stars with the fear of mortal physical death. We strive to move beyond the confines of our known existence yet clutch grudgingly to the routines of our lives. This tension between the 'polar opposites' drives us onward in our search for understanding – sometimes taking risks that uncover new qualities from within and sometimes stopping along the way to consolidate the gains which were achieved along the way.

This brings us back to the problem of language and the fact that, in its present form, language is often constructed upon the lines of how we perceive reality. Therefore, language tends toward describing the world through dualism (subject-object interplay) and materialism. Every time we say "go *there*" or "see *that*" or "bring *this*" we reveal – and *reinforce* – our belief that reality is constructed of separate and distinct objects, locations, activities and more. We continuously testify to a world of separation and reinforce that perspective to our consciousness. Even more so is this perspective reinforced when we speak about each other as distinct objects by employing the labels 'I', 'you', 'us' and 'they'. While language serves a valuable role in connecting us to others it also upholds the perception that we are separate. A new approach to the use of language will be needed in order to bring forward a truer sense of our relationship to each other and the Divine.

Some instances of this can be seen within cultures where the emphasis on the separate "I" was less pronounced. In these cases, the culture in question often possessed a keen aversion to concepts that bind consciousness to time and space. Many amongst First Nations peoples in North America lacked a conceptual framework for separating themselves from nature and the land. Because of this, notions of 'partitioning land' or 'transferring the ownership of land to others' has been generally nonexistent. This artificial fragmentation imposed a new way of 'relating' to the land as though it had now somehow become separate from them. Until this idea was forced upon them by European settlers they had largely seen themselves as an integral part of nature. A separation of this sort was sacrilege and affected the very foundations of their identity.

Another interesting example of language and identity can be found in Tibetan culture. This unique language is believed to have no known origin nor belong to any other language family. Tibetan culture is grounded partly in Buddhism and its philosophy of the illusory nature of the personal self. One interesting feature of this circumstance is that the Tibetan language is 'ergative' rather than 'accusative', as is found in English. Tibetan employs the use of a thematic subject rather than an individual agent as its subject. Therefore, rather than saying "I am going to the city", as we might in English, a Tibetan would say something that translates along the lines of "going to the city is being done by me". What dominates grammatically in the sentence is the unfolding theme or event of going to the city while the individual who is doing the "going" is merely one aspect of many aspects in this larger event. In fact, it is not unusual to read long passages in Tibetan describing a variety of encounters and events only to discover near the end which character or person was involved in the narrative. Such rendering of the storyline has the particular psychological effect of diminishing the importance of the personal

"I" whilst maintaining the unique characteristics or activities which the participant might lend to the account. An interesting shift in perspective might be offered to the reader could they but, for some measure of time, remove themselves from being referred to as the central character of their own life and imagine themselves as only one aspect of a larger unfolding tale. Our psychological reflex, particularly in the west and under the influence of the English language, is to describe events from the perspective of the individual – as if this perspective was the only one (or most important one) available to be told. The approach in Tibetan, as emerging from a more de-centralised point of view, is certainly unfamiliar in western society but might bring new and striking insights regarding our emphasis on "I" as the predominant subject in western languages and society.

Language is central in our ongoing communication and integral to our further evolution. It helps us to define who we are and how we understand ourselves to be in the world. But it can be as much a prison as a path to liberation. Our current challenge is to understand that humanity is rapidly beginning to grasp the fact that it is fundamentally interconnected as one with each other and with the Divine. Our language, however, is steeped in the attitude of separation, competition, fragmentation and opposition. Not only do we need to evolve our vocabulary we also require a new way of speaking and communicating that can reflect the ever-growing awareness of our wholeness and interdependence. What is required is a language of nonduality and oneness.

Suffice it to say that a form of language sufficient to reflect the essential unity of all has not yet been developed for common usage. Until such a time, the language of duality will have to suffice – albeit with its clumsy phrasing, paradoxes and contradicttions when attempting to present nondualistic themes. Perhaps this limitation in itself will spur humanity on to discover new ways to reach out to one another that do not rely on reinforcing the separation between subjects but, rather, enhances the unanimity of existence and synthesis of the Whole. The advent of this new understanding about ourselves is the needed impetus for such discovery.

Unity and Individuality

> You are your own teacher.
> Investigate yourself to find the
> truth—inside, not outside.
>
> – *Ajahn Chah*

There is probably no greater possession so treasured by human beings as the 'sense of personal selfhood' or *individuality*. For the individual woman or man it represents *the* defining edifice by which they might be known and recognised as existing in the world. Without individuality there is no contrast or understanding of distinctiveness amongst a world of "presences". In a landscape of subjects and objects individuality is the way in which consciousness can be known by others as unique and it is through the development of these observable qualities that it can stand out in society and function (well or poorly) in the world of form.

Individuality is an essential development in the process of evolution and is the growing congregation of qualities and characteristics which increasingly articulates the *quality* of consciousness. While the nature of consciousness may be universal and wholistic its unique forms of expression down through the various planes of manifestation often appear fragmented and incomplete. Over time, further attributes and properties develop for a person, create havoc for a time, and eventually become balanced and integrated within their overall expression. Thus, the development of individuality can be seen as the growing capacity of the indwelling consciousness to express the qualities of its nature in ever-increasing detail and variety. The more accurately it can reflect its fuller nature through whatever pursuits or activities undertaken the more whole, all-inclusive and balanced will consciousness demonstrate itself in the world.

According to the esoteric teachings consciousness seeks to know and then express itself in its fullest measure. As such, the development of individuality is paramount in achieving that end. Through trial and error in everyday experience consciousness acts through its vehicle of manifestation and continues to assimilate and further modify its character depending upon its capacity to recognise and comprehend the consequences of those actions. Subsequently, individuality grows both over the course of a lifetime and through successive incarnations. In some instances, qualities arise which are revelatory for the individual. At other times, experience can lead to the development of characteristics which result in further alienation, fragmentation or self-centred behaviour. These selfish attributes cause suffering for the consciousness and, eventually, result in adjustments that can modify its expression toward exhibiting more wholeness, inclusiveness and balance. The difficulty for consciousness is that the process is largely undertaken blindly. There is no cosmic instruction manual for spiritual growth and knowledge is often gained through the action and reaction in the world (karma). From "the seeds you sow, so shall you reap", thus garner the results that can guide future actions.

Suffering is the result of wrong action and wrong action is the result of wrong (or insufficient) understanding about the nature of reality. Much of what consciousness determines about itself and the world is derived from the manner in which it registers and perceives the form world. That perception occurs almost entirely through the physical and emotional senses and so the world is presented to the indwelling consciousness as actions and reactions between objects in the material world. What is not perceived or understood is that consciousness is in everything and that its own individualised portion of consciousness is not separate or disconnected from the whole. Therefore, it is governed by spiritual laws which are not wholly discernible to modern material science. With this wrong interpretation of the world consciousness proceeds to build its qualities of expression in terms of being a separate form. As a result, it unwittingly functions in a contrary manner to the oneness of reality.

If consciousness could perceive 'reality-as-it-is' it would more readily develop characteristics of fairness, equality, sharing, cooperation, non-violence, harmlessness, unity, coherence and more. Established social systems would be designed to sustain the needs of all equally and harm toward others in any manner would be unthinkable. Commonly practiced social values would be to "love one another as yourself" and to "do unto others as you would have others do unto you". More than simply cherished aphorisms, these ideas would finally be recognised as the spiritual laws which govern our evolution on this planet.

Unfortunately, the present general state of awareness does not easily afford the capacity to perceive reality as it truly is. The full array of physical and emotional senses communicates a perspective of material separation. Rather than constructing a harmonious society based on synthesis and unity, consciousness struggles to compete with others in a system designed to reward competition, scarcity and division. National, racial or generational characteristics arise which are the result of these distorted perceptions and the 'individual' is encouraged to be self-serving in many of his behaviours and activities. This deepening isolation and alienation leads to anger, violence, greed and, ultimately, more suffering. Once this framework has been established for the indwelling consciousness a sort of perpetual feedback loop is set in motion – with whole societies caught up in the struggle to maintain dominance or security within this wrong interpretation of reality. Suffering inevitably leads to adjustments in behaviours, both individual and societal, but the process is painful and unnecessarily slow. This suffering could be significantly 'softened' where the individual or the community could determine to make changes that dramatically alter the orientation of society. We have seen such groundbreaking changes in events like the development of new economic systems based on equality, human rights movements, the emancipation of slaves, or in the creation of great documents like the Magna Carta and the American Constitution. Each advance brings to the population an increased liberation and expansion of individual expression leading to progress for following generations.

The significant challenge facing each individual today is to develop a broader understanding about the oneness of reality to a degree that it can become our standard worldview. Through the use of the rational faculties more and more people are beginning to understand that the picture of reality presented through the senses is incomplete and that, despite appearances, reality functions as a unified and synthetic whole. More importantly, a critical mass of people must begin to collectively act along the lines of the principles and conditions which exemplify a unified world. While this seems a difficult task at first glance the movement is already underway on a massive scale, albeit not fully coordinated or harmonised. Throughout the world today we see a gathering of the forces of millions of individuals marching for peace, justice and equality. The essential unity of life is an idea that has taken hold amongst populations everywhere and it has breathed new life into the collective consciousness of the planet.

This brings us back to the discussion of individuality and its value (or limitation) as a vehicle for expressing the nature of consciousness. Consciousness, being itself of the inner nature of oneness, must build in the material world a vehicle for expressing that oneness. Practically speaking, that personality vehicle should be grounded in a worldview that appreciates the unity of existence in order to stimulate those wholistic and inclusive qualities of expression which are inherent in consciousness. With an acceptance of oneness and unity the individual can seek to make space for those qualities and structures in society and everyday life. As the outer expression more accurately reflects that nature of the indwelling consciousness so, too, will suffering diminish. The inner world and the outer world align and, as a result, life itself becomes increasingly harmonious.

It is also important to bring to light another critical point. Individuality need not be a separating factor for consciousness where it is understood as a mode of expression for wholeness rather than as an instrument of self-aggrandisement. That is, if the indwelling consciousness can redirect the purpose of individuality along the lines of selflessness and service then the person can come to experience an entirely new relationship with the world around them. Where consciousness had previously formed this notion of separateness, 'individuality' was a tool for benefiting oneself in the world through an entirely centralised point of view. However, where consciousness can de-centralise itself from the belief that it is a separate entity then individuality becomes a mode of expression wherein the indwelling consciousness can act more consistently for the benefit of society and the Whole. This notion may be unfamiliar to some at first since our minds have been conditioned to see our individuality as though it was the boundary which only defines our separation and self-centered activity in the world.

It might be useful to take a closer look at our earlier analogy of consciousness as an ocean representing the Whole. The interconnectedness of the Whole remains hidden under the surface of the ocean and what we observe above the surface in the world of 'forms' is the multitude of waves, each in their own unique shape, size and

Unity and Individuality

movement. Consciousness, because of its limited tools of perception, has only been able to see the individual waves on the surface and therefore believes that its own existence is merely one of these waves amongst the multitude of other individual and waves. One wave crashes against another, or enhances another, or opposes another. Each wave can only relate to one another by the unique activity that the others exhibit on the surface through their shapes and activities, and this perception conditions each wave to define itself according to the distinct qualities that they, themselves, have on the surface. At this stage in the analogy consciousness has identified itself with the individual attributes of being a separate wave and has defined the boundary of its 'self' by those individual features. It has identified with its individuality as existing amongst other individual appearances.

Let us imagine now that the wave becomes aware of the deeper ocean below the surface. It becomes aware of the fact that no matter how unique it can make its expression and movement on the surface it always remains an inseparable part of the source of its existence in the world. With this new awareness, the identity of consciousness necessarily changes. The unique and individual form of the wave remains in expression but a new understanding of its relationship to the larger ocean unfolds. It comes to understand that its fundamental nature is the ocean and that its individual appearance on the surface is only a momentary and unique expression of that underlying nature. It does not lose its form on the surface, or its effect on other waves, but the orientation – the identity – has shifted from being the separate wave to being part of the Whole. The individuality of the wave no longer defines its identity and a definitive de-centralisation begins to evolve. The wave no longer serves it own separate purpose, as formulated through its previous self-centered and limited experience on the surface, but begins to serve the greater purpose of the ocean from which it now knows it is part. In this analogy we can begin to see how individuality can remain as an integral expression of the outer form world while no longer being the defining object of identity.

Currently, for most people, individuality is one of the defining features of personal identity and, therefore, leads to separative activity. However, if consciousness could come to understand itself as part of a nondual whole then individuality becomes a vehicle of expression through which the next great step in human evolution could unfold. Humanity today demonstrates the achievement of individuality. In fact, one might argue that we have overemphasised the importance of individuality to the extreme of approaching a type of hyper-individuality. So great is the prominence of self-serving individuality today that the world appears imperilled by its dominance in every aspect of society. This 'cult of individuality' is dangerous since it appears to have no self-governing throttle and can only serve to pull humanity further apart from one another unless some greater uniting factor can be brought to bear on the multitudes of differing viewpoints. Individuality today functions throughout the world as if it were the very goal of life itself. Thus, individuality has had no higher activity to pursue beyond further amplification of itself as the centre of its own world. It has become its own goal. This has caused the development of individuality to mutate into rampant *individualism*, where the influence of material duality has exaggerated the drive to promote and overstate one's uniqueness and place in the world. Lacking an understanding of the need for individuality to work in harmony or synthesise with the Whole life becomes a pursuit of hedonistic self-affirmation and self-satisfaction. Where the development of individuality could be viewed within a larger awareness of a unified reality the indwelling consciousness would employ its unique individual expression toward benefiting that Whole. This is really only common sense and one must ask how further we believe humanity can travel down the road of individualism before the entirety of civilisation collapses into exclusionism, hyper-alienation and the utter breakdown of all social cohesion.

The good news is that a global shift is already underway and many around the world understand that we live in a world that is interconnected and interdependent. The realisation has now begun to dawn on the minds of millions that the way forward is through equality, justice and sharing. Despite the challenges that face a civilisation that has been constructed on the principles of competition and separation, enormous progress can be seen in every avenue of society today. While it is true that younger and future generations will develop a nondual ethic more easily where it is presented to them at earlier stages of life there are many now within every generation who are rapidly awakening to the need for unity. Given efforts toward a less distorted worldview, a rehabilitation of the world away from greed, selfishness and violence could be rapid and unrelenting in the coming years.

It remains for us to look at one last question on this topic. In what way could the development and expression of individuality possibly lead to peace? That is to say, how can individuality be used as an instrument of unity, harmony and synthesis in the world? Personal identity as we know it today is largely informed by the perspective of duality and separation. Therefore, our individual characteristics and traits are necessarily seen as something to be cultivated toward the acquiring advantages for ourselves and those close to us. However, as we have intimated in the discussion so far, it may be possible that consciousness can possess both an expression of its individuality while still retaining awareness that we are connected to the Whole. Alice Bailey points out in *A Treatise on Cosmic Fire* that:

> Yet, though we are merged with the whole, we do not lose our identity, but forever remain separated units of consciousness, though one with all that lives or is.

Our identity is forever subject to growth and expansion and exists as the 'idea' that we have about who we are. During childhood, identity changes through to adulthood and then further evolves to old age and beyond. Each morsel of experience, subtle or gross, adds to our understanding of ourselves and the world we live in and contributes to that 'form' which we call identity. This identity forms, in time and space, the limiting structure for the indwelling consciousness. Liberation, as that notion stands as a goal for the evolving consciousness, is really liberation from the ring-pass-not or boundary of one's present confining identity and into another which is greater and more all-cncompassing.

Identity always exists in any moment and at any stage as *that immediate idea of what we believe ourselves to be*. Regardless of the degree to which transcendence of identity is achieved by consciousness there always remains some greater identification. As each new identity is created, that expanded version provides the new boundary for consciousness. All the while, the individuality and individual qualities are refined and expanded to both benefit by, and contribute to, further growth of identity. But what happens when awareness begins to identify with a belief in all-inclusiveness and a nondual reality? What is the result if an individual is taught from the outset that they are only part of a larger Whole to which they are interconnected and interdependent? There is no reason to believe that any aspect of individuality or individual expression will be lost. On the contrary, only the purpose and meaning for that individuality would change radically. That is, the purpose for individual expression would now be dedicated to benefiting others and the world around us.

To some this might seem like an unusual proposition. It might appear abnormal or bizarre that the gift of our individuality should be turned primarily outwards to the benefit of others rather than focused on increasing our own lives. In our culture of "be all you can be" (presumably for your own success) and "live the life you want" (according to your own pleasure or gratification) such an edict to direct the entirety of your individuality toward the

Unity and Individuality

advantage of others or the Whole seems counterintuitive or misplaced. However, hasn't this been the central message in virtually every spiritual precept for the last five thousand years? The Buddha taught compassion to all living creatures. Christ demonstrated an entire life dedicated to helping the poor, healing the sick and aiding the dispossessed. His injunction was to become your brother's keeper. Mohammed encouraged a life of peace and service to God's creation. These all have made essential the offering up of one's unique gifts and abilities to the benefit and sustenance of fellow human beings. Is it possible that we have simply been so immersed in our own self-absorption and self-development that we could not seriously entertain a total and unreserved reorientation of our individuality toward helping the world around us?

Returning to individuality, we can see that individuality is not, in itself, a particular problem for humanity insofar as it can represent a unique note of quality or characteristic for the indwelling consciousness. However, when those features become focused through the lens of separation and self-serving purpose individuality becomes a noxious and divisive element which poisons our relationship with the world around us and suffuses experience with fear, insufficiency and despair. Thus is born the social perils which are narcissism and hyper-individuality, and likewise follows their companions of war, destruction, injustice, hatred, racism, sexism and violence.

Are we one or are we separate? Your individual answer to this, if honest, foretells the path upon which your life and experience is likely to unfold. Beyond that, having declared your perspective, are you prepared to live within the terms of those beliefs? If you believe yourself to be fundamentally separate from others and the world, are you prepared to truly manifest *that* reality and its consequences for yourself? If you believe yourself to be fundamentally interconnected and interdependent with the world, are you prepared to truly manifest that reality and its consequences for yourself? The consciousness, as always, has free will to decide and, from that, to experience disharmony or harmony, suffering or joy – whatever be the results of our actions.

A further point in this self-reflective exercise is to recognise that if you don't much concern yourself with either position, or if you are not committed to understanding the implications of this inquiry, then your consciousness is likely to default back to the world view which is being fed to it through your senses. Without some *intention* to expend or expand the effort needed to move beyond the current limits of our present conditioned consciousness the tendency will always exist toward settling back into the sensory experience of material dualism. We are beings of divine consciousness con-

Unity and Individuality

strained by the limits of our material vehicles and pacified into believing that we are nothing more than separate entities. Nothing short of an internal revolution and effort will enable each of us to 'break free' from the imprisoning condition within which we find ourselves. In order to bring suffering to an end one must grasp onto the notions of unity and build a demonstration of that into every waking moment of expression. Initially the work feels arduous since it requires 'swimming against the stream' of one's own daily conditioning. Over time, however, daily life and a new sense of reality can begin to organise itself around this principle and invoke nourishment from the inner life. There is nothing more embracing and life enhancing than living your outer life in direct alignment with the very nature of your being.

The challenge, then, is whether the individual can develop an identity which strikes a chord which resonates with the unique qualities of the undivided consciousness – a quality which is the Soul's privilege to express. Moreover, can it do so without that unique expression crystallising into a rigid identity which permits of no further expansion? In other words, can an individual demonstrate a fuller measure of that individuality without *attaching* to that expanded individuality as a new fixed and permanent identity? Can the indwelling consciousness utilise the qualities of expression which make it an individual actor in the world but not become identified with those characteristics as some sort of *permanent* 'self' – for it is this vision of a permanent self which constitutes, again, the chains by which the consciousness is bound to suffering.

It is this idea which Shakespeare so clearly attempted to communicate in his famous monologue from *As You Like It*:

> All the world's a stage,
> And all the men and women merely players;
> They have their exits and entrances,
> And one man in his time plays many parts...

He goes on in this passage to describe the seven stages of a person's life, as consciousness passes from one performance to another through life, donning one persona here and another there until the round of life is complete. The danger which constantly threatens the actor (as well as the consciousness) is that he completely forgets that it is only a role that he plays. The indwelling consciousness in life comes to *believe* that they are the role, the temporary identity. Can you imagine the trials and tribulations facing the actor returning home yet still carrying the additional burden of the role they could not leave behind at the theatre? And so much the worse is that the happiness or sorrow, the benefit or tragedy, which befalls the character on stage also informs the fate of the actor themselves. What relief it is for the actor who can return home at the end of the day and set aside its theatrical self. Even more so, you can imagine, is the relief for consciousness which has achieved a detachment from the self-created identity in the material world.

So can we have individuality without individualism? The answer is 'yes', although it surely requires a reorientation from what we have come to know as the normal separative worldview in society. It may seem impossible to some that we could be individual and yet not devote those characteristics toward self-interested pursuits. Almost every aspect of modern society seems fundamentally designed and motivated at achieving the pursuit of one's own interests. Every facet of our existence – from the acquisition of food, housing, education or healthcare to the establishment of security, reputation or social relationships – seems to be governed by the individual's capacity to achieve those interests largely for themselves. Competition for the basic needs of life is an approach that infects our workplaces, community structures, academic institutions and even religious lives. One can hardly start the day without facing some circumstance where self-interested pursuits are the central theme. Not only is such a world grossly inefficient and barbaric in its functioning but it is also absolutely unnecessary. It arises out of a fragmented understanding of reality and is perpetuated by the further divisions that it impresses upon us. As Krishnamurti correctly asserted "it is a form of violence" and this misuse of individuality forces us to perpetuate that violence against one another.

Is it possible for us to imagine a world where the pursuit of individuality and individual expression remains an important part of our unfolding presence in the world yet operates almost entirely on behalf of the benefit and welfare of others? Can our self-interest be turned toward supporting the needs of society and the Whole? The spiritual crisis of our present age requires that we face these questions and our survival on this planet demands that we come to the correct conclusion. Will we be able to overcome the advance of narcissistic self-aggrandisement and transform our world to one of global solidarity, wholeness, justice (fairness), sharing and love? Surely, the end of suffering is within our grasp.

The Economics of Unity: Sharing

> Right human relations is
> the only true peace.
>
> – *Alice A. Bailey*

Since the premise of this book is to establish unity as the fundamental basis for life and living it is only fitting we examine the area of economics since commerce and the exchange or distribution of goods and resources is critical to civilisation. In fact, commercialisation and the commoditisation of virtually every aspect of our lives have reached a point where it now threatens the very capacity to sustain our continued existence on this finite planet. The appetite for money and profit has become the primary goal of life for many, exceeding our basic appreciation for quality, sustainability, environmental and ecological stability, social justice and even our own safety and mortality. Dis-unity has been both the fertile soil as well as the fertiliser for this dystopian pursuit of power and profit. Nowhere has this dis-unity played a more tyrannical and subjugating role in our lives than through the economic sphere of life. So much is this the case that the pursuit of money, in order to secure the most basic of needs for life, dominates the lives of virtually every person on this planet. This pursuit necessarily enters into every relationship and, therefore, colours every interaction. If the essence of relationship is unity, then the pursuit or over-valuation of the acquisition of money will almost always negatively contaminate relationship as it manifests in society. This point cannot be over-emphasised.

For a better understanding, and to establish a wider platform for discussion, let us attempt to simplify the ideas and the language. The word 'economy' comes from the Greek *oikonomos* (*oikos* = "house, abode" + *nomos* = "managing") to mean "household management". Later, it was extended further to take on the meaning of "frugality or judicious use of resources". Economics is, at its most basic, an activity leading to the efficient or frugal management and distribution of goods and resources.

In terms of the individual, this involves an appreciation of one's own resources alongside the aim to use those resources in an efficient and sustainable manner. For all intents and purposes this can be reasonably simple since the range of options usually applies to the individual's immediate environment as well as the securing of their own basic needs. As we extend the arena of economics to include societal, national or international interests the logistics of economics can become extremely complex, although the goal does not really change.

The Economics of Unity: Sharing

The frugal management of resources is still directed to securing the basic needs of a society, nation or global community in order that its members can grow, develop and flourish. This eventually expands to include higher and more refined needs. As the initial most basic needs such as food, water and sanitation are secured those greater needs can then also be pursued. Education, healthcare, shelter and security become the further aim. As a society secures those social needs other important goals come into view and include art, science, religion, philosophy and, most importantly, spiritual development and self-discovery. Circumstances such as high population densities, displacement of age groups, and the accessibility or availability of local resources and infrastructure require the implementation of economic systems that can adjust for those changing circumstances. The management of social resources (from which individuals draw their own personal resources) can be accomplished through any approach which seeks to identify a fair and balanced distribution for all and then modeling the function of the economy to fulfil those needs equally. On the other hand, a bias toward a particular individual or entity as the exclusive or specialised agent for the redistribution of resources can advantage some individuals or sectors of society over others. As this occurs, those individuals who do not receive special status or advantage can begin to be seen as a liability against the distribution of resources for the advantaged or preferred few. Economics then becomes perverted to serve the needs of various special interest groups and the original purpose of economics is lost. It is no longer a process of fair management of resources for everyone but, rather, the apprehension and domination of those resources as a means of maximising welfare and wealth of a privileged few. In this 'turning' of economics away from being a beneficial social system and into a tool for growing individual wealth, economics can become a dis-unifying force that can achieve nothing but further fragmentation, isolation and alienation.

History has evidenced a wide range of economic systems, each growing out of the general awareness of society at the time. Each system has brought, for a time, relative stability and security to the society within which it arose and laboured to demonstrate both the strengths and shortcomings of their individual approaches. Likewise, each has exhibited an inevitable decline, imbalance and period of instability. The deterioration of every system has led to a period where the supply of resources and their distribution became captive by a select individual or group of individuals who, maximising their own positions, upset the balance of that system. Such is the history of human economic development. At this stage in the discussion it is important to make two fundamental but related statements which might add a fresh or revealing perspective on our discussion. Firstly, regardless of any view we might have developed previously, *economics is synonymous with relationship* and, therefore, is deeply associated with the values that we hold about relationship. Good relationships are informed by trust and other altruistic values between the relating parties while bad relationships are informed by distrust, ill intentions or selfishness. Economics is nothing more than a means of relating to each other where the medium of exchange is not conversation or friendship but is represented by the resources that we have to provide to one another.

Secondly, *the basis upon which we form relationships with one another is informed by our worldview*. Most importantly, whether we view the world as a duality (as subjects and objects) or as a nonduality (as all part of the One) will the basis upon how we relate to one another. Our worldview serves as the grounds upon which that relationship will be manifested in our social systems, whether that interaction be friendships or economic relations. It is the incorrect and distorted belief of separateness which has led to the collapse of past economic systems and which continues to inform the injustice and imbalance in today's current global system. Grounded in the view that we are each and all independent agents, the current stage of capitalism has produced some of the greatest examples of injustice that we have ever seen in history.

These two points merit further expansion and there is no better place to start than with the notion that *economics is synonymous with relationship.* It might help to illustrate this idea through the use of another simple thought experiment. As we pursue this idea together let us try to avoid some sterile setting devoid of humanity and personal contact. I was always suspicious during my years in university of economics professors who started every introduction to economic theory with the statement "All things being equal, etc, etc...". I soon discovered that this was a convenient caveat that allowed economists to separate economic theory from the real human interaction and relationship – which is *never* "equal". It also provides the grounds through which economic transactions might find a way to proceed while devoid of fairness, compassion or ethics. I would go so far as to suggest that we should try to view economics as a sub-discipline within the fields of human psychology, ethics, sociology and anthropology (no insult intended toward the economists in the room). Economics is an expression of human relationship, interaction and motivation. Therefore, let's attempt to enter into our thought experiment so as to create within it a personal living experience from which could arise honest human reactions from out of our moral senses. It is often much easier to make ideological pronouncements (or, especially, denouncements) when peering out at the world through some distant and foreign theorem. But let us be confronted by our own experience in which we feel personally responsible for the consequences of those circumstances and we are bound to be more serious and thoughtful about the how to approach the situation. Every action we perform in the world is personal and will set in motion positive or negative consequences that come back to us. This is the Law of Cause and Effect (Karma) and it makes everything we do *very* personal. It is naïve and self-deceptive to think that economics and economic relationships could somehow receive a pass to operate outside of these fundamental laws of life.

Imagine, therefore, that you are a merchant in today's world of comercialisation and the present elevation of market forces as one of *the* central principles behind economic efficiency. You own a small shop in the marketplace and you are solely responsible for the survival of your family (let's say a spouse and two children) through the sale of your products. "All things being equal", you typically follow the rules of "supply and demand" and you set your prices according to "how much the market will bear". When demand for a particular product is high then you charge more and when demand for a product is low you must reduce the product cost as much as you have to in order to continue selling it. You purchase your wares through a local wholesale supplier and re-sell these products for a retail profit to consumers. Let's further assume that you purchase your products from a wholesaler for one unit of local currency which is then multiplied by a "reasonable" factor before you sell it to the public at a profit. You have determined that you need to sell your products for at least twice what you paid for it just to cover your basic overhead costs of rent, utilities, wages and other necessary costs. Your "profit" is then the result of whatever you sell your products for beyond your basic costs. The numbers in this case don't particularly matter since they still follow basic "principles" in economics and are sufficient for our needs in this experiment. The principles of market forces allow you to charge as much as you wish on the retail side as long as the "market will bear it" and consumers continue to purchase your product. This is true even if the profit achieved is 10, 20 or even 30 times the wholesale cost of what you needed to earn in order to pay your basic costs. What the "market will bear" is dependent upon many factors which include the general wealth of the local consumers, the presence of other competitors in the market selling the same product, and other factors which will have some moderating pressure on how much you might decide to charge for your wares. We have now created a simple scenario which is sufficient for our purposes. It does not matter what details we might wish to adjust in the construction of this setting since these are only technicalities that are irrelevant to the main factor which will be the focus of our inquiry. In the end, you are selling a product from which you are making as high a profit as possible relevant to the myriad of external factors (keeping in mind that if you weren't making a sufficient profit then you wouldn't stay in business for long).

Now imagine that you are at your shop one day when a stranger enters your establishment. She examines the various items in your display and inquires as to the price of each, which you report as 20 units per product (remember, you only need to sell it for 2 units to "break even" on your costs). She contends that she only has 20 units to spend and feels that your price is too high. You point out to her that the same product is available at another merchant's shop but that their price is also 20 units and that this is the "going rate" for these items. Since she determines a need for this item and can afford it she makes her purchase for the full price of 20 units of currency. This type of activity continues and at the finish of your day you have sold a useful amount of product. In this instance, you have benefited from "market forces" which have allowed you to maximise your profits based on market conditions. You have moved your wares to numerous strangers who were all in need of your merchandise.

What you have not factored into the day's work is the multitude of personal human interactions you had and how much you might have 'disconnected' yourself from the 'livingness' and 'in-the-moment' experience of interacting with your customers. You do not know the personal circumstances of each person and you do not know the challenges in life that each face individually. Nor do you have a clear idea of the complex motivations behind why they came into your shop. You do not factor in their current level of depression or anxiety and you do not calculate the amount of hours that they had to work in order to make the funds that they gave you. You do not need to make any effort to understand their behaviour or existence, and there was no necessity to validate your fundamental 'connectedness' with them. In every instance, your transaction took precedence over almost every other factor within these interactions. That is, you could discount all humanistic factors within each relationship which might have caused enough interference in the encounter to adjust the price toward something that more readily suited *their* circumstances. This is not to say that you did not have various emotional feelings toward each individual who entered your shop – some people you like, some you dislike – but you had the luxury of not having to engage with the human aspect within each interchange.

We justify this 'distancing' in many ways by saying things like "it's just business" or "if I give this person a deal then I have to give everyone a deal". But regardless of our reasoning we are rationalising the fact that we can look at the other person through the lens of separation. The encounter can be devoid of meaningfulness other than as a source of income for our transaction. We must acquiesce to this need to redefine the other as a mere 'consumer' since we are bound to the blind instruments of market forces. Those market forces dictate that the consumer first become a secondary factor separate from us so that we can justify our disengagement from their needs and amplify our own in the exchange.

Some might feel uneasy with the characterisation of a market economy in these terms. It appears cold and dehumanising. Nevertheless, this is the ground upon which a material view of the world forces us to relate with one another. The basic fact in present western economics is that market forces are blind and, within themselves, have no particular ethical or moral constraints. The market economy rests on the beneficial effects of egoism and the only natural constraints within a market economy are the automatic limitations that arise through having competing egos. In order for you, the shopkeeper, to function willingly in this indifferent landscape you will need to reduce the 'other' to a mere 'factor' of the transaction that does not include all of the other messiness of being human. This is why individuals must rely on the capacity to offload any sense of personal responsibility for their human encounter under the justification that they are merely fulfilling 'economic principles' or 'economic activity'. What has to be downplayed in current economics is that the participating parties had a full human interaction and that every economic interaction is really a moment of human relationship. This is why consumers can often feel so betrayed when they discover that prices are being fixed or artificially inflated. There is a sub-text of trust between two human beings during an economic transaction which feels to have been subverted or violated in some way when the consumer discovers that the transaction has been misrepresented in some way. It is not enough to say that "this is just business" and whole industries have been created around verifying the trustworthiness of businesses.

Trust is not a feature of business. Trust is a feature of human interaction, although it often becomes confused with business. It is important to begin to see the looming connection to our premise about the underlying unity in these examples. We cannot choose to simply deny the existence of interconnection and interdependence in select areas of life and not suffer the consequences that it will generate for us. Economics, first and foremost, is relationship and the values or principles of relationship are really the true factors that we must consider. If we are fundamentally not separate, then to live honestly we must develop a form of economics which values and reflects that interconnectivity and interdependence.

Now let's go back to our thought experiment and imagine a second visitor to your shop. This time the customer entering your shop is a close friend of twenty years. You have been through many experiences together and value her friendship deeply. Her husband recently lost his job so you know that they have been under significant financial pressure of late. You talk for awhile about the difficult times and she explains that they are in great need of the product in your shop but only have 15 units to spend on the 20 unit item. She inquires whether you could see your way to selling the item to her at a discount for the 15 units. You think about her circumstances and also know that her youngest child has been sick recently, placing even greater financial burdens on their family. You really see them as a close extension of your own family and you feel compassion and empathy toward your friend. Looking at the situation you decide that it might even be more helpful to them if you would give her two products for a total price of 10 units. You know this is far under the regular sale price and far below what price might be dictated by market competition but your sense of responsibility in the relationship to help someone with whom you feel deeply connected easily outweighs blind market forces, even while you recognise that you will still be receiving your basic expenses plus a small profit. What has happened in this instance which can account for this new outcome even in the midst of what admittedly may be any number of beneficial (to you) market 'conditions' and 'forces'? This new factor, of course, is that you cannot separate your humanity – your love and friendship – from someone that you experience an affinity with.

In both versions of our thought experiment the rules of market forces provided for the same range of possibilities and outcomes in either transaction. However, it was the act of evaluating each relationship which in the end defined how the transaction unfolded. In modern commerce, our disconnectedness with one another is often so immediate and automatic that we are unaware that we are doing it. Where we become aware that we are in the presence of a closer relationship and have the capability to alter the terms of the transaction then the interaction takes on a new dynamic. You see this most obviously in barter-based communities where each transaction is negotiated under an assortment of both spoken and unspoken factors. What you remain intimately aware of is that you are bartering with another human being with common human interests and needs. So much worse to have to point out that many in western society today do not understand that their behaviour toward an economic transaction is representative of their behaviour in relationship with other human beings. How we treat our "customer" is reflective of how we are willing to treat other human beings in a relationship. This principle holds true whether we describe the economics between two people or between political blocs, corporations, races, genders or nations. Is there any wonder why our world economy is in such turmoil at this time?

We can say, then, that where an appreciation for connectedness to the 'other' exists in any relationship so, too, can the essence of that relationship be conveyed in their economic transactions. Alternatively, the absence of accountability or responsibility toward one another will express itself in our economics through the qualities of alienation, untrustworthiness, injustice and competitiveness. No matter how many scenarios you play out in our thought experiment it is the actual *quality* of our sense of connectedness or interdependence which will determine the quality and outcome of the economic interaction.

The Economics of Unity: Sharing

Economics is a synonym for relationship and 'right economics' is necessarily related to 'right relationship'. Said differently, you cannot create a system of right economics – demonstrating fairness (justice), sufficiency and sustainability – without the possession of right relationship based in mutual respect, connection, appreciation and love for one another. Where two or more distinct 'actors' exist so, too, will their economic interaction be determined by their understanding of the underlying unity of their nature.

Some have argued that human beings are inherently competitive and that greed is fundamental to our nature. Yet, this does not appear to be true outside of the artificial political, economic and religious systems that we have created. These systems are often intentionally designed to enhance the experience of separation or isolation and, therefore, to undermine the natural interdependence that we are capable of spontaneously manifesting.

An easy illustration can be made in this regard. The 'family unit' is recognised as one of the most fundamental and important expressions of relationship in society. Under any ordinary circumstances, we instinctively express unity and interdependence when in the family structure. The economics of the family unit is inherently one of love, sharing, mutual sacrifice and common security. In its day to day function and basic principles it is difficult to compare it with any existing mainstream economic model that we see today, although it is fair to say that the basic function of the family unit exhibits strong parallels to some main principles in socialism. The family unit is composed of our most cherished forms of relationship – the unconditional distribution of resources for the benefit of all, the self-sacrifice demonstrated by parents for their family, the nourishment and encouragement from parents to their children, the happiness and engagement between siblings, and so much more. We recognise these various traits and characteristics as the minimal requirements for a healthy and sustainable family life. Yet it does not seem to register for us that these factors of relationship should also be carried forward or extended into all of our social relationships, including economic relationships.

Important and sustainable relationships often involve a degree of sacrifice undertaken so that others within the relationship can grow to reach their own individual potentials. These sacrifices are not random, but are determined by a deep and abiding understanding of the real needs of 'others' coupled with a willingness to unconditionally share the fruits from a common pool of resources. This is the bedrock of trust in the family dynamic and stimulates reciprocal love and cooperation. Altogether these qualities and more come together to produce security and resilience in the family unit. These characteristics of sharing, self-sacrifice, love, nurturance, trust and protection arise naturally and are only limited where some member becomes imbalanced with regard to their individual needs above the needs of others in the group. The more strongly the spirit of self-sacrifice and mutual respect manifest, the more stable family unity becomes. This stability radiates outward from the core and spreads out in some measure to other close relatives – perhaps to grandparents or aunts and uncles. It can also be extended beyond the inner circle of family to include some neighbours or the community. It can even spread to other groups of 'like mind' (religious, political, etc) and stretch out beyond city precincts, national borders or continental boundaries to enrich others in need around the world.

The present danger to this family dynamic occurs when individual members reach out beyond the margins of family life and engage with a contradictory socio-economic system. The individual is now disposed to participate in a relational system based upon competition, greed, selfishness and inequality. They must progressively, if not rapidly, adapt to a world that is both isolating and alienating. These challenges force the individual to integrate into the world of pursuits contrary to those principles of love and care which dominate within the family unit. Influences from each 'world' spill over into each other's domain causing dissonance and disaffection. New and disruptive traits are introduced into the once stable family systems and the resulting instability negatively affects the larger social matrix. Relationship within the family is turned on its head and this schizophrenic existence can introduce disconnection and hostility into the home life.

This brings us to the second point stated earlier – *that the basis upon which we form relationships with one another is informed by our worldview.* This links specifically to whether we understand the world to be a field of separate and distinct entities or whether we accept that our nature is One and that humanity exists as an interconnected whole. The first and most persistent contact between our consciousness and the world around us is through our senses. Almost everything that we can immediately perceive about reality is delivered to our experiencing consciousness as a series of sensory impulses which describe the world as material and object-filled. What those material senses reveal to us are only those portions of the material cosmos which are vibrating specifically to that narrow bandwidth of energies detectable by those sense organs. It creates for us an image about the world of a subject separate and apart from other subjects and objects.

This is what philosophers, theologians and mystics throughout the ages have referred to as "The Great Illusion". This is 'dualism" and it presents our consciousness with a very real problem. Not only do our senses provide us a *partial* view of the world, they also generate for us a perspective and worldview which is, itself, a further alienating factor to the mind.

Herein lies part of the problem for humanity. We have not found a way to operate wholeheartedly in the world as if it were nondual and whole. We default to our sensory experience even though we have definitive proof that nature is wholly interdependent and interconnected. The nature of reality is one and so, too, is the nature of humanity. "All things being equal", such a view of the world should naturally result in behaviours affirming or reflecting that truth. What we need to work toward now are the ways in which we can live together in the expression of nonduality and oneness. Social systems would obviously need to be organised to express the qualities of interconnectedness, unity, universal access, non-violent sustainability, harmonious interactions, peace, mutual respect, diversity and freedom. Even more so should these qualities and characteristics be found in our economic systems since this is often the more common instance upon which much of our relationship with one another is expressed.

The concept of sharing is not unfamiliar amongst a variety of religious traditions as well as many indigenous and aboriginal

The Economics of Unity: Sharing

communities. Economic interchange is often expressed as a type of communal activity related to the ethic of caring for one another in a world animated by one original creative force. If the evocation to "love one another as yourself" is the ideal to strive toward then sharing the world's resources with one another would be the most natural and efficient demonstration of that. If we accept that the nature of humanity is one then the only sane path forward *is* to treat one another "as if" we were each other's support.

Under this worldview the only rational economic model would be one grounded in the principle of sharing. The Bible is replete with verses extolling sharing as a way forward for humanity. Although it is emphasised repeatedly, verses from Acts 4:32-37 can serve to present one of the clearest examples.

> 32 All the believers *were one in heart and mind. No one claimed that any of their possessions was their own, but they shared everything they had.* 33 With great power the apostles continued to testify to the resurrection of the Lord Jesus. And God's grace was so powerfully at work in them all 34 that *there were no needy persons among them.* For from time to time those who owned land or houses sold them, brought the money from the sales 35 and put it at the apostles' feet,

and *it was distributed to anyone who had need.* (emphasis added by the author)

There are two important points to note here. The first is that the Christian ethic repeatedly emphasises that sharing carries a stamp of approval by God and that right relationship is expressed through a social economy that is first and foremost based upon that principle of sharing. At least as far as the Christian ethic is concerned, right relationship and right economics are presented as an economic system of sharing and the equal distribution of resources. This is not merely a program of philanthropy benefitting a few poor here and there but is expressed as the fundamental economic practice through which to administer a fair and sufficient distribution of resources throughout society. It is hard to identify any society today where the principles of sharing provide the fundamental basis for social sustainment and it is heartbreaking to know that a more substantial system of global sharing could easily prevent the current suffering of billions of impoverished people in the world.

The second important point to note from the earlier passage is that the principle of personal property ownership – which our social and economic systems today treat as sacrosanct – was rejected in many earlier societies. In the example just cited, any instance of land or property ownership was generally liquidated and the proceeds given over to the benefit of the community. This speaks to the principle of not only right relationship toward one another but also right relationship to the earth and to the Divine.

The idea of being able to "own the land" is simply another illusion that we attempt to pass on to ourselves as truth. Of course we can create any number of belief systems that applaud the ownership of land and we can all agree to follow that belief as we would any political or religious idea but, in reality, there really is no way to divide something out of the cosmos and claim that it is solely ours. Even though we draw imaginary lines around a perceived plot of land it still partakes of the air, the weather, the growth of plants, the life in the soil and more. The belief in the *primacy* of ownership belongs to the type of economic system that espouses separation and isolation. The notion of owning personal property is a right that *we give ourselves* and it is only valid within the terms of our willingness to hang on to that belief. It is only an idea.

The illusion of 'land ownership' is widely recognised by many indigenous cultures and spiritual groups around the world. Swami Vivekananda, for example, spoke of the poisonous effects of personal ownership and possession: "With the sense of possession comes our thought of selfishness, selfishness brings on misery".

The Economics of Unity: Sharing

The virtue of sharing is recognised throughout various teachings as one of the highest forms of personal expression and social interaction. So powerful is its effect on others in society that it is often described as having the power to vanquish enemies and restore justice to society. Hindu tradition exalts in the cultivation of *dāna* or *daana*. A Sanskrit word, *dāna* connotes the cardinal virtue of generosity or giving to others. It is seen as an essential attitude to achieve on the way to attaining liberation. It also acts as an inoculation against personal selfishness and self-centredness. A familiar Hindu passage states that "Living creatures get influenced through dānam; Enemies lose hostility through dānam; A stranger may become a loved one through dānam; Vices are killed by dānam". As an important element in establishing social stability, eliminating poverty and reducing violence the practice of giving and sharing is arguably the politician's leading tools in securing social order and balance. The importance of this is described unmistakably in the Mahabharata:

> An assurance unto all creatures with love and affection and abstention from every kind of injury, acts of kindness and favor done to a person in distress, whatever gifts are made without the giver's ever thinking of them as gifts made by him,

constitute, O chief of Bharata's race, the highest and best of gifts (dāna).

Buddhist practice recognises 'giving' as one of the first characteristics for which the disciple must strive. The Buddha taught that giving and sharing should be done without the expectation of any reward or benefit to oneself and, if so undertaken with spontaneity, produces tremendous merit and progress for the seeker. The power in giving comes from the fact that it has the capacity to free you from the sense of isolation and alienation. It intimately connects us to the world around and invokes within us that aspect of the self which is already interdependent and interconnected. When we share unconditionally we can literally experience that sense of oneness that we are in the world. In the *Avadana Jataka*, the Buddha speaks of the unmistakable effect of sharing:

> If living beings knew the fruit and final reward of generosity and the distribution of gifts, as I know them, then they would not eat their food without giving to others and sharing with others, even if it were their last morsel and mouthful. If they should meet a person who is worthy of receiving a gift, selfishness would not abide in their hearts.

The Economics of Unity: Sharing

Herein lays the challenge for humanity at this time. We have created a very extensive and entrenched economic system based on greed, selfishness and competition. The average person is deeply integrated into that structure and it has a deeply corrupting influence on human nature. As a result, in the world today, billions of people are without the very basics needed to live a dignified life. Wars rage across the globe, violence marks the headlines of our daily news while fear and anxiety dominate the lives of many. Where a sane individual desires peace and security, we seem to have created the exact opposite for ourselves through a competitive scheme of personal acquisition that leaves us more alienated and isolated by the day. How can we transition from an economics of selfishness to an economics of sharing? How can we change our collective approach to the world in a way that no longer leaves us separate and untrusting from one another?

The answer is really quite simple and within the grasp of everyone. The solution is in knowing that the only effort required on your part is to personally begin now to make the shift toward sharing. Many individuals postpone participating in the economics of sharing, opting to join in only once they see (most) others involved. The thinking here is that no real or sustainable benefit for themselves can be secured until the majority of society become members of the sharing economy. Many would like to share but nobody wants to be the first to do so whilst still in a system that values the acquisition of money as the principle "need". Under these conditions, it is thought, that sharing could threaten your very own state of security.

This entirely misconstrues the nature of sharing as well as how sharing and service to others might function effectively in our society. We tend to interpret our notions of economic exchange through the current capitalist model of self-interest and individualism – how can I obtain the needed financial security to make my life happier. If we are honest with ourselves it is not money that we are seeking but, ultimately, it is *happiness* that we seek and we see money as the means by which happiness will be secured. That message, however, is flawed. Money can purchase our basic material needs in a capitalist system (which, when examined carefully, are really very insignificant) but it cannot buy us the happiness and sense of fulfillment or purpose in life for which we are genuinely searching. We have been made to look at life as a series of transactions which yield profits or gains (mostly monetary gains) which can then be used toward acquiring some nearly infinite offering of "things" from thc marketplace. This marketplace, consequently, has been grooming consumers to believe that their particular products will fulfill that search for happiness and wholeness. We resist the act of sharing as part of a workable system of economics because the act of sharing does not appear to provide the immediate returns needed to continue buying one's way to happiness.

This is not how sharing works. Sharing elevates economic transactions to a higher octave and makes human relationship and the value of human life and living paramount in the exchange rather than the acquisition of profit or material advantage. It fundamentally bypasses the need for the 'middleman' to happiness (i.e., money) and pays its dividends immediately and directly in the currency of happiness and fulfillment. The interest on the investment in sharing is collected instantaneously by both parties in the transaction with the receiving party acquiring an item of need (food, clothing, etc) and the Good Samaritan obtaining instant satisfaction, happiness and a sense of fulfillment.

The only amounts that you need to share are those resources which you might have already dedicated toward purchasing your happiness from the marketplace. Any amount that you might have spent on acquiring 'things' to distract you from your loneliness and alienation can become a potential resource for sharing with those in need. The goals of happiness and fulfillment are achieved much more effectively and efficiently.

The Economics of Unity: Sharing

Sharing in the sense that I am discussing here is not a method of exchange where both parties receive equivalent material resources. One party receives an important item for their basic material security while the other receives the gift of a meaningful and enriching experience. A further benefit derived by both parties is the shared experience of connectedness, inclusion, mutual respect and love. This experience carries an even greater benefit since the 'externalities' of an economic exchange based on sharing or service includes deeper social cohesiveness, increased empathy and compassion between people, improved public security, enhanced cooperation and a societal framework defined by its altruism and mutual wellbeing. A social agenda based in a practical and realistic appreciation for sharing and service, in support of the needs of each other, would represent the first major steps for humanity toward establishing a lasting harmony and peace in the world. It signifies the manifestation of a way of life which embodies the unity and interconnectedness of the human family and creates the necessary conditions for the elimination of war, famine, poverty and disease.

The pursuit of personal possessions can never provide a sense of sustained fulfillment and happiness. In fact, the pursuit of possessions almost always leads to an increase in stress, obligation, compulsion, liability and confinement. When asked to seriously consider sharing our resources to create a more fair and balanced society we often pull back in the fear of diminishing our own needed physical assets or it is perceived as a threat to our own capacity to be happy. The cost we have paid through the belief in obtaining happiness from the pursuit of material gains has been to tolerate isolation and suffering as a shadow that dims the light of our daily experience. This is the spiritual crisis that we, the human family, face today and has become corrosive to both our communities and the environment. Without sharing, economics remains defined only by material exchanges and withholds from us the human element of kindness and compassion that we so crave in our daily interactions.

The reward of sharing is sharing itself. There is no other activity within the realm of economics that can bring a human being more rapidly to their goal of achieving inner happiness. The act of sharing connects us to that part of ourselves which is whole and loving. We don't share in order to gain security. We share because it is an expression of our nature and it brings us into alignment with the source of who we are.

In her work *Destiny of the Nations,* Bailey states that "Peace will be the result of understanding and sharing, and not the origin of them, as the pacifists so often imply". Sharing pays its dividends of happiness immediately and a life of sharing

The Economics of Unity: Sharing

"pays back" to the donor a lifetime of true happiness, fulfillment and purposefulness. A day of sharing is a joyful experience and an economy based in sharing builds that entire ethic into society and into our everyday lives. Time and again we experience the value of sharing in small ways, yet have been made to fear implementing that as a central activity in our daily lives. We can make a clear choice for our lives. On the one hand, we can live an entire life working and struggling to earn enough money to buy the things that we think or hope will make us happy but which can only really provide temporary moments of fleeting pleasure. In the end we will look back at a lifetime of acquisition, fear, anxiety and insecurity and wonder why we didn't spend more time just engaging more honestly and generously with others. On the other hand, we can take the most efficient route and immerse our lives in the experience of giving and serving to others. The end of such a life is filled with a treasure trove of happy memories and reflections upon a life filled with purpose, meaning and happiness – a life of heartfelt unity and belonging.

A life expressed through service and sharing can be challenging to initiate from within a society that lacks trust. One might ask, "who should share first"? The answer, again, is simple. *You* should share, and share now, and share often. It does not mean giving up the important or primary resources

The Economics of Unity: Sharing

that you require in order to sustain your own basic needs. You need only give of those excess resources which might have been used to find your happiness in the marketplace. Someone has to share in order to begin the development of trust within society. You do not share in order to get something material in return. You share in order to benefit another who is in need of the resources that could advance their lives. You *may* happen to receive material items in return but the real treasure in sharing is the affirmation of connectedness that you receive. It is an affirmation of a correct understanding of your relationship to one another, to nature and to the Divine. You share in order to alleviate the real needs of another or to bring benefit to the world around you. Your happiness comes in living a life of right relationship to one another and in experiencing that connection and sense of belonging. The sharing economy, locally and globally, is the path forward for humanity and our delay in getting there perpetuates not only the suffering of others who need our help but it prolongs our own suffering in the world. This 'secret' of sharing has always been the cornerstone of poorer communities and I have never found generosity more abundant than when amongst the poor. They have already understood the power of sharing to deliver happiness and strengthen the foundations of community.

The Economics of Unity: Sharing

One of the main factors preventing justice within of society today is our collective lack of conviction around the oneness of humanity. It is my sincerest belief that we have now entered an era where those first steps into an expression of unity as a global family will be taken. A great movement toward understanding nondualism and humanity's interdependence is now underway and is proving to be the turning point toward a new and more egalitarian approach to living. This can particularly be seen in both the new experiments in the sharing economy as well as the rapidly disintegrating structures of the old competitive economics. I am very encouraged and optimistic about the voices rising in the world today on behalf of greater justice and equality. Even more heartening is the knowledge that the new economics does not arise out of factors that can be contained or determined within existing economic structures. The change is arising out of the expanding awareness of humanity and so there is nothing from within the field of the current economics which can halt its eventual emergence into the world. We are on the threshold of that new world and the courage to bring that world into manifestation requires only that you engage in sharing. The benefits are beyond description and provide the means to end suffering on our planet.

Unity: The Way Forward for Humanity

> In those moments when we forget ourselves—not thinking, "Am I happy?" but completely oblivious to our little ego—we spend a brief but beautiful holiday in heaven.
>
> – *Eknath Easwaran*

A fair measure of ground has been covered in looking at consciousness as the nature of who we are as well as the divine medium through which we are all interconnected and one. This consciousness dwells within each of us and provides for us, according to the distortions of our own personal identity, a capacity for awareness of who or what we are. Consciousness creates its vehicle out of the various 'materials' from the physical, emotional and mental planes. Consciousness then identifies itself with these temporary vehicles and, along with an admixture of assorted beliefs and ideals, becomes enmeshed with the material world through many lives. The resulting experience provides not only for the richness of civilisation but also the suffering that arises from its mistaken identification as a separate being. All actions made from this separative outlook eventually result in pain and disease for the vehicles. Many mistakes are made and a high price is paid by the personality as it persists in its journey to know and understand the nature of its true inner self. So, too, are great benefits accrued along the way with a gradually unfolding realisation that not only is the universe one Divine Whole but that the inner consciousness (the Soul) is also part of that Whole. The consummation of this long sojourn results in a series of achievements over the imprisoning effects of these physical, emotional and mental shackles leading to an eventual liberation and emancipation into a fuller knowledge of the Divine Self.

But is that the end of the story for human evolution? Does the journey end at the achievement of self-awareness? Certainly, a purely human-centered or individualistic perspective would contend that the individual has fulfilled its purpose through achieving liberation from its previous separate state. To achieve knowledge of one's own ultimate 'Self' is a great attainment for the individual little 'self', but of what benefit is that for the universe? After all, the universe is not here for us. We are part of the universe and, as such, must fulfill some position or role that makes the universe whole. Having come this far in our evolutionary journey do we not then have some role that this expression fulfills some expression within the larger Purpose of

Cosmos? It is perhaps hubris to believe that the whole reason for humanity's existence is for each individual to simply know themselves.

Such a conclusion, after all that has been discussed, would negate all of the valuable ground that we have covered. For one thing, any goal or purpose that might be ascribed to the individual or isolated Soul itself would be erroneous since we have already established that consciousness is an integral and undivided part of a Whole. Therefore, the Soul could only be part of a purpose which the Whole seeks to fulfill – hence those final liberating words "Not my will, but Thine, be done". Secondly, the liberating achievement by any individual in fully manifesting their inner divine nature is not a representation of the goal of the individual human being but, rather, a feat achieved in spite of it. As a whole today, humanity and its civilisational structures are largely fragmented, self-serving, overly competitive, individualistic and driven by fear and scarcity. A disciple working toward unity and liberation must do so within the challenges inherent in the present selfishly-oriented social (dis-)order.

So the real goal for humanity as a whole – for any legitimate purpose for humanity could only be manifested as a demonstration of its nature *together as a whole* – would require bringing forward the reality of that inner unity into complete expression. It should be clear by now that anything nearing an ultimate expression or purpose for human beings must incorporate all dimensions of their being – including the spiritual dimension. If the nature of humanity is unity and oneness then that collective expression must come into full display before any true purpose for that unity can be further unfolded. Like the individual disciple who must first bring forward those divine qualities which will eventually be employed to manifest their individual achievement, humanity as a whole must collectively manifest its nature as a unified whole in its day to day affairs. This means that the human family must become an expression of unity, cooperation, and right relationship in all of its activities including politics, economics, religion and all the other facets of civilisation.

This is no small task and, for many, achieving this may seem impossible. Our current discord makes the attainment of a fully unified society distant and problematical. Yet we have witnessed the steady march of mankind's progress throughout history as societies explored the limits of material advancement and developed a complex understanding of human inter-relations and justice. There is no doubt that a deeper understanding of our path ahead will eventually come to fruition and the signs of our growing collective awareness at this time speak to a period of enormously rapid progress once the tide of civilisation turns. We are now at that moment in history.

Regardless of the challenges, the demonstration of unity represents humanity's immediate goal ahead before the Purpose of that manifested unity can be revealed and unfolded. In this sense, unity itself is not the ultimate Purpose for humanity but merely the demonstration of a collective spiritual principle which is needed in order to express our greater destiny in the Cosmos. Having achieved unity, humanity will then be free to demonstrate aspects of Divinity which are the purview of Those who have achieved a synthetic relationship with the unfolding Will or Plan of Cosmos.

In *Esoteric Psychology Volume II*, Bailey provides an outline for humanity which hints at the potential future in store for a civilisation that will eventually express that full measure of collective unity. What is important to recognise is that the role set forth for humanity in the far distant future cannot be interpreted in terms of individual participation but speaks to a responsibility that humanity will shoulder as a Whole both within our solar system and beyond. The value of bringing this to our attention now provides us with a glimpse at the potential for humanity once we have achieved a particular stage of planetary synthesis and universal justice. Reviewing these statements also helps to put our own individual journeys into perspective and to know that our individual goal is to be a part of a much greater demonstration within the Purpose of Cosmos.

Bailey recounts four basic objectives that "Workers with the Plan" have set for Themselves in developing the future potential of the human kingdom. These objectives are general in nature since they only mark the approximate aim of their work as it relates to the possibility for human evolution. That these goals are still far beyond humanity's current state of expression should not hinder us from attempting to envision the possibilities that a unified planetary life might offer us. These four major goals are described to us in this way:

> 1. The first aim and the primary aim is to establish, through the medium of humanity, an outpost of the Consciousness of God in the solar system. This is a correspondence, macrocosmically understood, of the relationship existing between a Master and His group of disciples. This, if pondered on, may serve as a clue to the significance of our planetary work.

> 2. To found upon earth (as has already been indicated) a powerhouse of such potency and a focal point of such energy that humanity—as a whole—can be a factor in the solar system, bringing about changes and events of a unique nature in

the planetary life and lives (and therefore in the [solar] system itself) and inducing an interstellar activity.

3. To develop a station of light, through the medium of the fourth kingdom in nature [the human kingdom], which will serve not only the planet, and not only our particular solar system, but the seven systems of which ours is one. This question of light, bound up as it is with the colours of the seven rays, is as yet an embryo science, and it would be useless for us to enlarge upon it here.

4. To set up a magnetic centre in the universe, in which the human kingdom and the kingdom of souls will, united or at-oned, be the point of most intense power, and which will serve the developed Lives within the radius of the radiance of the *One About Whom Naught May Be Said*.

The Masters hint further at an even greater possibility for humankind but that is so far down the evolutionary path that we are basically incapable of interpreting that opportunity within our present state of awareness.

Much can be written about the potential of humanity, yet it is of little use until we can overcome our immediate crisis and begin the process of manifesting the principles of sharing, unity and cooperation in our daily lives. Even the slightest movement in that direction at this time is being amplified by the new incoming influences on our planet and it is only a short time before we will start to see the first major expressions of a common Will to work together toward a better future. The way forward for humanity is through unity and the initial strike against the forces of separation, competition and commercialisation have already sounded the death knell for this outworn mode of living. The age of unity, brotherhood, cooperation and love has begun.

Unity and the End of Suffering

> Unity only exists in the heart. It is a feeling: love. And in love the notion of self disappears; only the other remains.
>
> – *Swami Prajnanpad*

It is sometimes possible to come away from a discussion such as the one we have had here without advancing our appreciation of an idea by any significant measure. A familiar idea, if examined only through the 'lens' of common experience may not necessarily yield a new insight for all. My attempt in this book has been to alter the lens through which the reader might have been accustomed to understanding the notion of unity and, in doing so, to make of this idea a living presence in the experience of the reader rather than simply another thoughtform, concept or belief. More than simply a hollow aphorism behind which we might rally or support, unity must become the fundamental living experience underlying every activity and pursuit in our lives. It must become the substance of our dreams, the ambition of our daily occupation and the law under which we take every breath of our being. There is no limit to the significance that it should, and will, play in the salvation of our species and our planet.

It serves a useful purpose, therefore, to utilise this final chapter to review those points which I have hoped to convey. Our journey has explored many features and uncovered diverse landscapes, sometimes demanding our sincerest attention. So it will not be a loss to stand back and look at the entire map in order to get a greater picture of the journey. Here, then, are the ideas concerning unity that I have hoped to convey:

1. *The Fundamental Nature of Reality is 'Oneness'.*

This statement is not intended to be interpreted in any trivial or sentimental manner. Both science (relativity and quantum mechanics) and religion (eastern and western traditions) have presented evidence and experience in support of this basic fact and we need to begin to see this as the nature of our existence – even if the world does not appear to us in this way. In the same way that we once accepted the existence of the atom even before we could observe it through the electron microscope, we must eventually take seriously that all of the material appearances and activities that we experience arise out of this 'oneness' principle. For some today, this notion is still hard to grasp. In the near future it will become a conviction as common in our thinking as the colour of the sky or the sound of a bumble bee.

2. *The Nature of Reality – Oneness – is experienced through our sensory equipment on the physical plane as material duality and separateness.*

Herein lies the problem, and challenge, for humanity and speaks to why the achievement of enlightenment or liberation is so difficult. It also explains why the idea of Oneness (nonduality) has been repeatedly overlooked or dismissed by some of the best thinkers. Our consciousness is part of the whole but because we experience the world through our physical senses we perceive ourselves as separate and distinct from other objects and beings. This distorted perspective tempers how we interact with others and, as such, further validates and ingrains the illusion of separateness so as to 'set it in stone'. This contributes to the conditioning factors in the mind which work against consciousness knowing itself 'as it is'. Rather than perceiving itself as part of the infinite whole, consciousness largely orients itself according to the limited viewpoint delivered through the senses. This leads to our next point.

3. *The Indwelling Consciousness naturally seeks to know and understand itself, and so it forms its identity from the thoughts, beliefs and experiences of the world. The identification with this 'thoughtform' (which is the personal identity) constitutes the prison walls for consciousness and solidifies and conditions the experience of separation.*

On the path to self expression consciousness must construct for itself some identity or persona through which to relate itself to the world and formulate its own unique expression in relation to others. Experiences gained through the physical, emotional and mental equipment help the indwelling consciousness to determine its own range of possible activities in the world along with the multitude of responses that these may elicit from others. As its existence unfolds over time, these expressions, strategies and beliefs about its own experience are brought together (often unconsciously) to form the *personal identity*. This persona, based upon the ever evolving experiences of the individualised consciousness, can be relatively fluid (as in the case of an easy-going flexible personality) or can be quite fixed (as in the case of a rigid or fundamentalist personality). Regardless of the quality of the persona, it provides the identity and 'vehicle' through which the indwelling consciousness will contact the world around it and facilitate its ongoing expression and evolution. What is important to remember is that it is not necessarily the characteristics of the constructed identity that matter as significantly as the fact that consciousness has *identified* itself with those characteristics. This identification with the constructed persona is what constitutes the prison or 'great illusion' spoken of so often in various traditions. It is the resulting experience of attachment to this separateness which is the root cause of all suffering.

Consciousness instinctively seeks to know itself, to express itself and to understand its relationship to the cosmos. Whether viewed in the context of one's own personal life or within some larger global or universal context, we seek to know where we belong. That process of orientation involves moving from experience to experience, expression to expression, thought to thought and to make from those some further conclusion about who we are. Some explorers may arrive earlier in life to an answer that satisfies them enough to quell the urge to look further for a time. They settle on some identity that seems to fulfill the spectrum of curiosity granted them in life. Others may continue on this exploration for their entire lifetime, spurred on by a deep dissatisfaction arising from the sense of a greater existence. Either way, the search for identity *itself* constitutes the very problem that generates the imprisoning factor for consciousness. That is, as soon as we find the slightest note of identity we have built the first prison wall. In its innate drive to know itself, consciousness identifies first with this, then that, then another – building for itself a progressively more complex 'idea' with which to align itself. But it is not the complexity of the persona itself which is the problem. Rather, it is the strength of its identification with that persona. It is literally the strength of the belief which translates directly as the strength of the prison walls restraining the indwelling consciousness and its capacity to see itself in some further or larger way. It is also why a period of 'identity crisis' in a person's life, where one has outgrown their current situation in life, can represent a sort of 'prison break' for the consciousness which can allow it to dismantle and then rebuild a newer, more comprehensive identity. The more comprehensive and inclusive each successive identity becomes the less inhibited it is to the expression of the fuller nature of one's own Consciousness (i.e., 'Oneness').

4. *Consciousness is on an evolutionary journey to first immerse itself in, and thereby identify with, dualistic matter. Later, through struggle and suffering, consciousness gradually liberates itself from identification with matter and masters the use of its various material bodies as vehicles of expression for*

the divine qualities of its true nature – which is Oneness.

Life and consciousness is unfolding in time and space through evolution. While not governed themselves by time and space, their identification with the various planes of matter and material existence make their expression subject to the limitations of time and space. The evolution of consciousness is not separate from the evolution of matter. In fact, they are intimately entwined and rely upon one another. Scholars in many fields have mapped the extensive evolution of life through the physical forms in nature – starting at the Big Bang and proceeding up to and including the profound diversity of forms that we see in the world today. But little has been recorded on the evolution of consciousness and the many forms it has shrouded itself on its journey of increasing expression up through the various kingdoms in nature. Such a study would quickly reveal the interplay between consciousness and matter, and that a moment of 'crisis' or destruction in the material world can often signify the release or expansion of consciousness from the limiting vehicles of form and matter. Whether we observe the sprout of a seedling from the seed, the emergence of a chick from the egg, the escape of the butterfly from its chrysalis or even the creation of the universe from the Big Bang itself we are similarly witnessing the movement of consciousness into some greater form and some greater expression.

5. *Thoughts are 'things' and constitute some of the forms which first enrich and later imprison the indwelling consciousness. For consciousness, thoughts are as real and solid as a brick wall.*

In the search to know itself, consciousness stimulates the expanding nature of the various forms through which it might express in increasing ways. In the mineral and vegetable kingdoms those forms may be a stone or plant and their stimulation can develop ever more beautiful shapes, colours or scents as a new mode of expression for the indwelling life. In the animal kingdom forms become more complex in order to express qualities of sentience, and even characteristics such as herd loyalty or devotion. The human kingdom represents yet another stage and opportunity for consciousness. 'Man' is the root word for the Sanskrit term *manas* meaning 'to think' or 'mind', and the human kingdom offers consciousness its first opportunity to build its identity consciously on the plane of mind – to express itself through the form world of ideas and ideals. For humanity, the path of evolution proceeds through the domain of thoughts and ideas but also provides consciousness with the opportunity to finally 'know itself' and to reason about that knowledge. Here consciousness suffers more and more from its wrong use of thoughts and ideas, and through the appropriation of a complex identity of ideas which are not real in themselves. It is not the thoughts, ideas and beliefs which are the problem for consciousness so much as it is its *identification* with those thoughtforms. In fact, as was also the case in previous kingdoms, that which was the imprisoning factor at an earlier stage becomes the liberating factor later on when rightly understood and employed. Thoughts, therefore, are the 'materials' used by consciousness during its evolution through the human kingdom on its journey to further self-awareness. Control over one's own thought life constitutes one of the final obstacles faced before achieving liberation into yet higher realms of experience.

6. *Imprisonment of the consciousness through the identification with separate identity causes suffering, and through suffering the consciousness is taught the illusory nature of identity. This eventually leads to liberation.*

There is probably no simpler and complete summation of the human condition than that declared by the Buddha in his first of four great Noble Truths, "Life is suffering" (the Pāli term used is *dukkha*, meaning

Unity and the End of Suffering

'suffering', 'pain' or a kind of 'unsatisfactoriness in life'). In his pronouncement on the agony facing humanity he identified attachment to the sensory experience of the world, including attachment to the illusory persona, as the cause of suffering. It is the illusion experienced by one's own Buddha-mind (the indwelling consciousness) which must be overcome. It was his great Brother the Christ who again demonstrated that it was the sacrifice or surrender of that illusory 'personal self' which could lead to liberation and a "life more abundant". The initial identification with the thoughtform of a 'personal self' brings with it, by definition, the experience of separation and alienation which can only be adapted and modified until sufficient suffering necessitates either the breakdown or abandonment of the process of unconscious identification. Therein lies the journey involving the sacrifice of those aspects or beliefs about oneself which, when seen for what they are, have been limiting the life and expression of the indwelling consciousness. Because this process is evolutionary the individual suffers while the various forms of identity are gradually released and overcome through time. When the indwelling consciousness becomes sufficiently aware of this recurring illusion and can break free of its attachments to the lower forms liberation into the next higher kingdom of manifestation becomes a possibility. The consciousness is freed to move beyond the boundaries of the human kingdom and can enter into the next spiritual kingdom – a state of awareness known by many traditions variously as the Kingdom of Souls, Nirvana, Heaven, etc. At that stage suffering as humanity understands it ends for the individual.

7. Unity cannot be brought about by any outer activity, but must be achieved in the inner awareness and inner state of being. Inner unity will automatically demonstrate as cooperation and right relationship in the outer world.

The source of discord, fragmentation and dis-unity is the personal mind and the way that it creates its personal identity. Once our consciousness identifies with that fragmented persona of a separate 'self' we begin to manifest that discord into our outer world. It is not enough to simply build more unified social systems in the world since we will still be participating in those from a disconnected and separate perspective. At best, we would be able to achieve some type of temporary cooperation, but never true unity. A true inner state of unity can only blossom for the individual when they can detach and 'stand back' from their mind and mental activities. One must learn to create a space between themselves (the consciousness) and their thoughts, emotions and physical body. In that condition of detachment, a state of unity is revealed within one's experience as having existed there all along. This inner unity can begin to guide the activities of the individual in the world. That inner landscape of unity, which is revealed lying beneath the separative activity of the mind, is an experience of wholeness and oneness.

8. The nature of consciousness is Love. Only in those briefs moments of detachment from the activity of mind can the individual experience true unconditional universal Love.

Humanity has been taught for long ages to "seek the Kingdom of Heaven within". This injunction is never more important than in the present day. The very nature of consciousness itself is that unconditional and unifying Love and the means to experience that is to develop an inner practice that seeks to 'stand back' or detach from the personal identity and its vehicles of expression. Inner practice, over time, can make the experience of one's own consciousness – and therefore the experience of unconditional universal Love – more accessible and permanent. This is the true revolution at hand in the world today and it is within the capability of each and every person.

9. We create our own emotional experience from within ourselves. It arises almost entirely from the filters and distortions of our own beliefs and attachments. We need to understand the importance of taking personal responsibility for how our identity modifies how we experience the world through our emotions and mind.

This can be one of the hardest notions for an individual to face. However, once accepted, they will have made a tremendous step toward the ending of suffering. It is the first stage in taking control of one's own individual experience as well as the process of achieving detachment of the consciousness from its vehicles.

We all face situations every day that give rise to an emotional or psychological response. How each situation affects us emotionally depends entirely upon how we experience it through the identity that we have created. Take, for example, a discussion between ten individuals on the subjects of, say, politics or religion. Each of those participants will react to that discussion depending upon how each of the ideas expressed relate to their own system of beliefs, ideas, attachments, aversions and more. The ideas do not change for any person but the reactions will vary widely depending upon each individual's identity. Each will come away from the event with an emotional reaction spanning the entire spectrum from happy or fulfilled to unhappy, disappointed or even humiliated. In another instance, such as a marriage relationship, one partner might continually express the need for more affection while the other is burdened by what appears to be an unquenchable thirst. How can there be such vastly different responses or interpretations for one single reality? It is because each participant is interpreting the experience through their own identity or 'filter'. The partner constantly looking for love or affection is isolated and alienated *inside*, and so no amount of actions in the outer world can (ultimately) resolve that need. Until that person can become centered and whole in their own interior being they will never be able to fully satisfy their perceived need through outer pursuits. If one feels unloved then one must find that love within. If one feels disconnected or alone then the experience of true connection can only be resolved by connecting to that aspect within themselves which is Whole. The "wants" of the personal identity are infinite and can never be entirely fulfilled – thus the capacity for the mind and identity to generate endless suffering. The way out of this trap is to learn to detach from the activity of the mind and emotions. This does not mean to bring an end to thoughts and emotions (although, that is possible too if sufficient effort can be spent in meditation). But one must end one's identification and attachment to those thoughts and emotions. By achieving detachment from the ever demanding desires of these vehicles one can step back from the suffering that they create within us.

10. *The goal of human relationship is the achievement and demonstration of Unity.*

It is abundantly clear that the formation of thoughts and beliefs about ourselves, and the subsequent *identification* with those ideas or personas, is the primary factor leading to the experience of separation, alienation and alone-ness. Gradually, as consciousness becomes aware that these identifications are, themselves, the source of that alienation a process begins to unfold which transforms the experience of alone-ness to all-oneness. The individual moves through atonement to at-one-ment.

Where an inner experience of separate-ness exists so, too, will that fragmented state get projected out into the outer world. At probably no other time in human history has civilisation demonstrated such disintegration, alienation and plain brutality against one another than it does in the present day. Not unlike the crisis facing any individual at the height of their own selfish behaviour humanity has brought about the conditions by which it could now experience, on a global scale, the most extreme forms of suffering possible from operating under the illusion of separation and exclusionism. Through the current global crisis humanity is being led to an unavoidable revelation that separation breeds chaos and destruction, and this discovery is rapidly bringing forward the circumstances under which a truer expression of its divine nature might emerge.

Already, global movements encouraging worldwide unity can be seen, promising to rehabilitate global institutions and bring together humanity under a common banner of shared goals and ambitions. Where right relationship to one another and to nature is perceived as interdependent and interconnected humanity will come to see that cooperation and unity must be employed throughout the fields of all human endeavour.

11. True Unity is an inner state of being. It is the experience when consciousness can detach from all of the interference or influence that arises in the physical, emotional and mental bodies. Inner Unity naturally and automatically results in outer cooperation and love.

The greatest achievements in our lives should be through the journey inside to know our true selves. Even without much striving we already get small hints from within that our nature is love and that we can feel compassion and empathy for others.

But we have been taught to look entirely to the outside world for any measure of 'achievement' and this completely blinds us to the treasure which lies right before our eyes.

It is true that our outer lives are projections or re-creations of our inner lives and a mind that is disordered or combative will live through that inner life to generate an outer existence that is disordered or combative. If you have an angry disposition (identity) then you will even try to overcome your anger in an angry way. As long as you are functioning through the vehicle of expression which is the problem itself you can only perpetuate (or even amplify) its qualities.

The solution is to 'step back' or 'rise above' the vehicle and find that space where you are the "observer" of that vehicle. Detachment from that problem body is the very first step in being able to overcome the challenges that it presents you. It is in this state of "observer" where total peace and unity can be experienced. Temporarily freed from the demands of the lower vehicles one's nature, which is love, can flow freely. In achieving increasing degrees of detachment an individual can experience increasing degrees of inner freedom and unity. This naturally and automatically becomes projected into our behaviours and activities in the outside world. This should not become a choice between whether we should live an 'inner' life or an 'outer' life. The aim of this discussion has been to show that we need to look inwardly for happiness and the nature of our being, and that this will then inform all of our outer activities as sharing, cooperation, justice and love.

12. *Individuality expressed by the personal ego leads to division and separation. Individuality expressed by detached consciousness leads to unity, wholeness and inclusivity. In these two different modes of expression, Individuality can be either necessary for evolution or an impediment to evolution – thus, the present problem for humanity.*

The long journey for consciousness begins in the ordered behaviour of the atom and progresses upward through the kingdoms of nature, expressing some aspect of its divine nature through successively complex forms. Each stage brings with it further achievements in differentiation and uniqueness. This process culminates in the development of a uniquely sophisticated vehicle of expression which we call *individuality*. This unique expression is capable of demonstrating those particular divine characteristics and the qualities of the indwelling consciousness. Individuality is critical to the continuance of evolution and the sum total of individual expressions eventually provides for the fullest manifestation of the nature of Cosmos. Every unique note is needed to complete the symphony. However, individuality also constitutes a major obstacle for the indwelling consciousness when it identifies with the particular vehicle of expression that it has constructed. This attachment to the developing 'vehicle of individuality' is also the cause of suffering for the advancing consciousness and can create temporary barriers to recognition of, and cooperation with, the Whole. The problem is *not* the development of individuality or individual expression – for that is a necessary outcome of evolution – but that the indwelling consciousness identifies itself with that individual expression and suffers as a consequence. "To be or not to be" is, indeed, the great Shakespearean tragedy undertaken by the Soul and the indwelling consciousness must eventually learn to "be in the world, but not of it".

13. *From the point of view of the personal ego or persona, Individuality is seen as a tool for personal aggrandisement and personal fulfillment. From the perspective of the indwelling Consciousness or Soul, Individuality is viewed as gift developed to be expressed for the benefit of humanity and advancement of the Plan of God.*

Unity and the End of Suffering

From the perspective of the personal illusory ego, individuality is thought to be the prime instrument by which to attain all that the personal desires deem necessary for happiness and security. Individuality is the 'tool' by which that persona interacts with the world to obtain the objects of its aims in life. The expression of individuality, in that case, will be determined largely by the particular beliefs and ideas which inhabit the confines of the illusory identity. In effect, the motive behind the expression of individuality will tend toward reflecting the motives of the self-centered and isolated identity. The expression of individuality will necessarily operate under the weight of a separative attitude. But what if the indwelling consciousness begins to see through the illusion of identity and starts to recognise the Whole of which it is a part?

Viewing itself to be an interconnected and interdependent part of the One, the aims of the indwelling consciousness take on a radically different colour. There is no reason to assume that individuality no longer functions, for that is the basis of manifestation itself. Rather, the expression of individuality takes on a new *motivation* and is forthwith put to use for benefiting the Whole. Individuality then becomes an instrument of the Whole, expressing the Will of Cosmos to which the indwelling consciousness has come to align itself. Individuality remains an instrument of consciousness but is now employed for the benefit of humanity and advancement of the Plan of God.

An interesting thought experiment is to envision such a time when you might see the use of your own individuality as an instrument for the benefit of the world rather than as a servant tasked with fulfilling personal needs and desires. Imagine a world in the not too distant future where whole populations see this same use for individuality on behalf of human welfare. For some, the idea of employing individuality primarily for others rather than for oneself seems foreign and incomprehensible. Nevertheless, it remains part of the forthcoming stages of development immediately ahead for humanity.

14. *While suffering is the fundamental 'friction' driving the evolution of consciousness forward it does not always have to be so to the extent that is witnessed today.*

While much of our individual suffering is the result of attachment to 'things' – most important of which is to our personal identity – it is conceivable that much of humanity will progressively work toward greater levels of detachment in the period ahead. Already we see movements toward minimalism and efforts to become less materialistic. As awareness increases, societal changes will also reverse the educational trends away from selfish pursuits and toward a more altruistic role in society. As sharing, cooperation and inclusiveness increase in the social fabric so, too, the degree of suffering that we see today will diminish. It is possible to imagine a time in the near future where increasing self-awareness can inculcate an appreciation for the benefits of global unity and this can serve to guide the individual along the path of right living and right relationship. Growth and evolution will no longer require the lash of alienation or the torment of loneliness but will proceed upon the healthier lines of self-discovery, expansion and identification with the Whole.

15. *Humanity has a role in the expression of the Purpose of God. However, it cannot undertake to fulfill that expression until it can first bring into manifestation a collective expression of its own nature, which is Unity.*

This statement, for many, can seem controversial. The question of teleology (attributing 'purpose' to phenomenon) is always dicey, especially when referring to humanity or God. It is not possible to ascribe any particular purpose for God or the Absolute. How could one even attempt to formulate something as mysterious and unfathomable as that? However, a certain degree of inference might be undertaken with regard to the purpose of humanity where the initial premise that the Universe is One is accepted. The reasoning is simple and follows what is hopefully a clear line of thinking. It begins with the notion that the universe as we know it is created in such a manner that everything is interconnected and interdependent within the Whole. Given that single premise, then it is possible to suggest that humanity is also One with all nature and with the Absolute (i.e, God) of which the physical universe is a manifestation. It also follows that whatever Purpose exists for that Universal Creator, humanity and all creation would be a part of manifesting or expressing that Purpose – however large or small that role might be from our perspective. Finally, whatever role that humanity will play in expressing the Purpose of God it would only be possible where humanity has itself achieved the fuller collective expression of its nature as Oneness. Unity is ultimately the destiny that humanity must, and will, achieve and in achieving that will demonstrate that aspect of the Cosmos which is its give. In short, the achievement and expression of unity by humanity will make it possible to manifest that aspect for which it is responsible within the greater Purpose of God.

Some might argue that I have engaged in somewhat of a circular reasoning in order to reach this outcome. However, I am not

Unity and the End of Suffering

attempting to prove an Ultimate Truth or First Principle. Rather, I have tried to lead the reader through the thoughts that I have laid out here to reveal the consequences of existing within a nondual Universe Whose fundamental nature is One. If we *are* One then the way ahead for humanity is through Unity.

~ ~ ~

If one could attempt to distill the contents of this book down to a few thoughts it would be this. The nature of reality is wholeness and we are an integral part of that oneness. However, our consciousness has come to identify itself with the activity of its vehicles – the mind, the emotions and the physical body. In this state of identification and imprisonment the world appears as a field of separate objects. Therefore, without any further insight beyond our senses, the unfolding of our lives can only be based in the divisive activities created by those separate vehicles of expression. The solution is to be able to see that we are not these vehicles but that we can use these vehicles to express the nature of our consciousness in a more refined and genuine way – which is Wholeness and Love. To detach from our vehicles does not mean we lose them, or lose control of them, or lose ourselves. On the contrary, this is the first step toward truly directing your own behaviours rather than them controlling your activities and reactions in life. This is true freedom and is the start of real unity in the world.

The nature of our mind is to think, and thinking involves breaking down the world into moments of isolated 'thoughts' about 'things'. The very action of the mind is to divide up the world around us and within us. This act of dividing the world and seeing ourselves as divided with it is part of the roots of suffering. Our consciousness, when identified with this fragmented notion of the world and who we are will then participate endlessly in that suffering.

The mind will always find a way to suffer. If you are not in a relationship you suffer over it. Once you get into a relationship you find a way to begin to suffer over it. If you have no job you will suffer over it. Once you find a job you will eventually suffer over it in some way as well. If you see that you lack any 'thing' you will suffer and once you acquire that 'thing' then it is inevitable that your mind will develop a reason to suffer about that thing. The mind will ruminate over both the having or not having of everything we experience, and so suffering is built into our experience from the start.

The end of suffering can begin when we start to end our attachment and identification with the mind and our vehicles of expression. To the degree that we can achieve a state of non-identification with the separate bodies will be the degree to which we will be able to become aware of our own inner nature – the Consciousness or Soul – which is completely whole and one with all of Cosmos. That state is unity, and it is within the reach of every human being to begin experiencing. While this unity presents a great challenge for consciousness – since it means reversing much of the conditioning that the mind has undergone – a single glimpse of that state of oneness can radically change the direction of one's life. In knowing that this state actually exists to be discovered within oneself, a world of unity can be rapidly brought about and established for coming generations.

Inner unity represents the end of suffering for humanity. The means to transform our world into a paradise has already begun. The larger work ahead will take decades, or even centuries, to bring about that universal experience of love. However, inner peace and a healthy measure of cooperation and right relationship can begin to take hold right now. It starts with the effort to step back from your vehicles and to know yourself as the inner observer of the world around you – including those temporary aspects of yourself that you have come to think of as your identity. The Kingdom of Heaven is truly "in you and all around you" but the challenge has been to work toward the seeing and achieving it. The perfect state of Nirvana is the only thing that ultimately exists except that we cannot see it while we are conditioned by our material vehicles and senses. These are not some far off locales which exist prior to birth or that we go to following death. They represent reality-as-it-is once you can shed the conditioning of the separative identity. You are separate from God because you *believe* you are. You are disconnected from the life of Nature because you are conditioned to think this way through the perspective of your senses. All of this can be overcome and, in successive stages, we can come to know again our true nature of interdependence, wholeness and love. This is the way forward for humanity and this can be the end of suffering for every individual on this planet. The choice to find that starts here.

www.ingramcontent.com/pod-product-compliance
Lightning Source LLC
Chambersburg PA
CBHW071705090426
42738CB00009B/1663